# It's Been Love All Along

## A Personal Revelation
## of the Father's Love

by
Zona Hayes-Morrow

17 16 15          10 9 8 7 6 5 4 3 2

*It's Been Love All Along*

ISBN: 978-160683-977-5

Copyright © 2014 Zona Hayes-Morrow

Published by Harrison House Publishers
Tulsa, OK 74145

# CONTENTS

# ENDORSEMENTS

Every solution and sign you seek begins with the revelation of God's love. Zona Hayes-Morrow has lived a life radically transformed and empowered by this revelation. Her story and the principles contained in the pages of this book will propel you into the depths of your Father's heart.

John Bevere

Author / Minister

Messenger International

Colorado Springs / United Kingdom / Australia

I am so proud of my daughter, Zona. A few years ago, she really experienced the love of Jesus in a supernatural way. That's what she wants to share with you in this book, It's Been Love All Along. I have walked through and with her during some of the darkest times that a human being could walk through but in the end, the love of our Father saw us through. Zona understands that wonderful unconditional love that cannot be quenched. You will be encouraged and uplifted as she helps you to draw closer to the Father and realize that nothing can separate you from the love of God!!

Dr. Norvel Hayes

# INTRODUCTION

Have you been struggling with a disease or a mental, emotional, marriage, family, or financial trauma that is continually repeated in your life? Do you want God's cure to be totally healed and walk in the peace of God? Love is God's remedy to every problem! The love of God will get rid of any demon and get rid of cancer or any disease. It will get rid of a confused mind. The true love of God will make the rebellious come back to God.

Before you can receive and operate in the things of God, you must walk in God's true unconditional love. Walking in the true love of God is the key to operating in the gifts of the Spirit and the fruit of the Spirit.

The love of God contains the answer to every question you'll ever ask for the rest of your life. It's food for your inward man. When you really understand that God is love, the works of the devil will never shackle you again. If you really understand God's love, you'll never wallow in the belief that you'll never amount to anything because of what you've done or said.

God is love! We all need to embrace these three words. You have to get a revelation of these three life-bringing words. The answer to every spiritual longing is to know the love of God and to know that God loves you. That is the answer to every mental and emotional dysfunction. It's the answer to healing for your body. God's is love—that's the way He is! This means that when you meet Him, you can say without a shadow of a doubt that God loves you.

# CHAPTER 1

## THE POWER OF GOD'S LOVE

*"And we have known and believed the love that God hath to us. God is love; and he that dwelleth in love dwelleth in God, and God in him."*

*1 John 4:16*

Do you really know what the love of God is? Do I really know what the love of God is? If we're too busy judging people, it is because we don't have enough love in us to love them. Salvation is more than just a ticket to Heaven. Salvation is the ultimate expression of love.

"God is love!" These three words contain the answer to every question you'll ever ask for the rest of your life. They are only three words you need to know to unlock all of life's mysteries. These words are food for your inner man. When you really understand these three words, the works of the devil will never shackle you again. If you really understand them, you'll never wallow in the belief that you'll never amount to anything because of what you've done or said.

We all need an understanding of these three words. You have to get a revelation of these three life-bringing words. The fulfillment of every spiritual longing can be found in knowing the love of God and the love God has for you. It's the answer to every mental and emotional dysfunction. In every case, it's the answer to the healing your body needs. God is love! That's what He is! This means that you can say without a shadow of a doubt that God loves you. Too many people think that this truth isn't earthshaking, but it absolutely is.

To other people, the truth that God loves them seems ridiculous. For example, I shared with a friend the fact that God loves her. She turned to me and said, "Don't be stupid Zona! How could God love me? I'm a worthless heap of garbage because of what I've done, what I've come out of, and what has been done to me. I am a worthless heap of garbage."

I revisited two girls I used to run with. One was ten years older than me and the other was five years older. One of the girls said, "I haven't found one reason in my life to believe that God could ever love me." My immediate thought was, *God is love – that's why He loves you!* However, I could relate to where she was coming from. Many of us have had thoughts like this at one time or another in our lives. Even if we haven't said the words out loud, we've had the thoughts.

When I was eighteen, I got on the wrong track. I'm sure glad there weren't computers, cell phones, and things like that back then. Had those things existed, the mess I made of my life could have been even greater. Sometimes, technology is just another demon to monopolize young people and lead them astray. During this time, I was certain that God did not love me.

I had many growths on my body. I hated those growths and begged my dad for surgery to remove them. I never thought about God loving me enough to remove those things I hated from my body. But my dad believed in the love of God for me and knew that God could remove those growths.

The growths disappeared on my body when my dad believed and paid the price by his unconditional love for me and his faith in God's love. They were there one minute and gone the next. The first thing I said when I noticed the growths were gone, while I was running down the hallway I grabbed my dad and said, "This is spooky business. You mean Dad, I didn't even do anything for God. You're the one who has been out winning souls, but still God loves me enough to remove growths off my body? One minute they were there and the next minute, they were gone. That's no exaggeration! They left in the twinkling of an eye." The unconditional nature of God's love amazed me!

Back then, if you were from a divorced home, you were considered messed up. Because I was being raised by my father only, many kids wouldn't play with me. Before they would play with me, my dad would have to reassure them that I did have a mother. Their acceptance of me was conditional. Because I wasn't like them, they often would not accept me.

When I'm talking about God's love, most people tell me they can't grasp what I'm saying. They decide they are not worthy of such love because of their past thoughts, behavior, and words. They feel like it would be presumptuous to say that God loves them. Other people try to justify themselves by saying that they did the best they could under the circumstances. Their logic gives them reason to believe they have earned the right to go to the good place after death. They never say, however, that their decency earns them the right to be loved by God. Is that the world we live in now, a world dominated by the belief that God only loves you if you're "decent"?

It is one thing to get to Heaven, and another thing altogether to claim a relationship with God. The world conjures up its own definition of "relationship" based on its understanding of love. Even sincere Christians often have a misunderstanding of what a relationship with God truly is like. They view their relationship with God like that of an examiner with a student. If they feel they've passed the test of accepting Jesus as their Lord and Savior, if they've properly said the sinner's prayer, they assume they must be in relationship with God.

It's true that Jesus died for us and that faith reaches out to receive Him personally, but there is more to the gospel than that. A lot of people who've said the sinner's prayer believe they will go to Heaven, yet they still wallow in a sense of worthlessness. They feel their lives have no more meaning than their neighbors' across the street who have no revelation of God's love for them.

Don't get me wrong, I want to make it to Heaven. But I also want to teach people while I'm still here on earth. I want to reach out to people and let them know that the gospel is God's announcement of His love toward us and what He's done for us. God is love! If I can teach people to truth of God's love, they will no longer live with a sense of worthlessness.

We all need to stay humble and love people where they're at. Share what God has done for you; talk about what God has brought you out of. That's the responsibility of every believer. The tragedy is that the gospel story is little known to many believers. They don't have a firm grasp of what the love of God truly is. Because they don't have a full understanding of God's love, they can't love other people no matter what. They only vaguely know that God loves them. They read the words in the Bible and they sing praise and worship songs, but the concept of the love of God is totally unrelated to the day-to-day world in which they live.

They may say, "I have to do this and that," and believe that is living out the Christian life. The truth is, you don't have to do anything but love God and let Him love you and love others through you. It's that simple.

God loves you. He loves you even in your sin. He loves you even if you're trying to be a perfect, self-righteous person. Many don't understand that self-righteousness is a demon sent from hell to steal the salvation of Christians right out from under them by giving them a hard heart because they're so prideful. God's love is unconditional – you can't make Him love you more, or less.

You see, we have many believers who have the same longing to be loved as the rest of the world. They live with the same anxieties in life as those who are not saved. In some cases, they even go to the same psychologists, psychiatrists, and counseling sessions as unbelievers.

Their understanding of salvation is limited to the knowledge that they will somehow escape hell by having said the sinner's prayer.

They believe God only deals with big issues such as judgment, damnation, repentance, and annual pledges to the church. They think that He's not the God of immediate concerns and He has nothing to say about the state of our minds or our stress levels. Everybody experiences stress. We live in a body. None of us are perfect. We yell, scream, and get mad. I don't care how spiritual or religious you are or how much you think you know; we all get that way.

Sometimes our stress level goes through the roof. Do you know how I work out my stress? I get on the Gazelle. When I'm upset, I get on my Gazelle exerciser. I don't do anything calm. I don't quiet myself to bring the presence of the Lord into the room. I don't do any of that. I get on my Gazelle and I walk and walk. After I get finished, I'm at the point in my mind and heart where I've walked off all my frustrations. Then I'm able to worship God and receive from Him. That is what I do.

When it's cool outside, you ought to see me walk the block. That is how I get out my frustration so I don't say anything that I'll regret. When I am talking on the phone, I will hang up to prevent myself from saying something I will regret. Empty words will hurt people. You have to understand that if you don't have anything to say but empty words, you don't need to say anything at all. You have to say words of life.

I went to lunch with three girls I hadn't been with for thirty years. One of them told me that she had the beginning stages of emphysema. I was there to speak life to her. I told her that I was there to see her and eat lunch with her because I love her and I was determined to speak life to her. Sometimes, just being in the presence of someone who loves you will minister life to you.

Life begins when we know that someone unconditionally loves us.

We are able to love God because He first loved us. Such unconditional love is the difference between Christianity and every other religion in the world. The entire Bible built upon the foundation of the words, "God is love."

Most people don't understand the nature of God's love. They wrongly assume that God's love us just human love taken to the infinite degree. You see, this is what we thought when we were children. The problem is, we never updated our thinking in adulthood because what we had done in our lives was so wrong in our own eyes. Everybody wants to blame their behavior on the devil, but the truth is what you have done was done because you chose to do it. It was your choice, and deep down we know that to be the truth. That's why we don't believe God could love ever us.

When I was eighteen, I didn't think that anybody loved me. I chose to look at God, stick my finger in the air and say, "God, I'll never serve You another day in my life—not ever!" I didn't understand that God's love is altogether different from human love.

We understand that a husband ought to love his wife and a mother ought to love her children. When we say that God loves us, we think of these types of love and believe that God's love is the same, only to a greater degree. When we use the word "love," we're talking about a love that appeals to the emotions or to the eye.

Have you ever noticed how the world judges people based on looks? When two women apply for a job, there may be one who is overweight who has a doctorate and another who is thin, looks like a model, but knows nothing. The majority of the time, companies will hire the slim woman. Then when they have to fire her because of substandard performance, they say they wish they had someone who knew what she was doing.

You have to understand that love is more than just the desire to possess the most desirable beauty. When you are truly in love with your husband or wife, their body, mind, and disposition excite you. I get butterflies if I know Terry is going to be there when I go home. The little imperfections don't matter. A husband can see the beauty in his wife and he can draw the emotion out of her. When you get married, you want to know you are loved in this way by your spouse.

Your love is ignited by who your spouse is to you. Terry makes my liver quiver. I like his personality. I like his disposition. I like his character. I like his eyes. I like his smile. I like his big shoulders. I like everything about him. There's nothing I don't like about him. I fell in love with him many years ago.

The word "fall" describes something that happens that is essentially beyond our control. For example, if we report that we fell off a cliff, we're communicating that we did not plan to do it. If we planned to go over the side of a mountain, we would have used the phrase, "I jumped off the cliff." Human love is not a choice we make, it is something that happens to us.

After my first husband died and went to Heaven, I never planned to get married again. I didn't even consider going on a date. I had people ask me to go on a date but I would say, "What? I don't think so." They would call on the phone and send gifts and I would tell my secretary to send them back. But then I met Terry and I could not help myself. We fall in love because of who the beloved is..

The problem is that millions of believers apply their human understanding of love when trying to comprehend divine love. They believe God will be swept off His feet by their spiritual beauty. Some people think that God will fall in love with them if they spend their days masking themselves behind religious rituals, sayings, and actions they completed to prove they are good. God does not fall in love with you because of all your hard work proving yourself to be good.

I once found myself in a cycle of confession that became my god. I wore myself out trying to do ritual confessions, only to realize that

I was worse off when I was done because my motive was wrong. I was saying the words but not letting God love me for who I am. He loves me whether or not I read a verse in the scriptures. He loves me whether I pray in tongues or not. He just loves me.

In my walk with God, the more I have realized that He loves me, the more I have been able to love Him as my hard heart began to get more flesh. After my heart of stone became more flesh, I was even able to realize that my mother really did love me as much as she could love me and with what she had. The revelation of the true nature of God's love for me enabled me to love others more fully.

I no longer had to go around thinking, *What did I do? Why did my mother not love me at five, six, and eight years old?* She used to look at me and say, "It's all your fault. This divorce is all your fault." I no longer struggled with wondering why she would do that. All my life, I took this history so hard - until I was 38 years old and came into a fuller understanding of God's love for me.

For many people, coming to Sunday church is like touching up their make-up in the bathroom. They are hoping that God will notice them and finally love them because they have come to church. There are believers living the Christian life, wondering whether they are still loved by God. They're afraid that God might be seeing through their promises and walking away in disgust. God will never walk away in disgust. We may leave God, but He never leaves us.

I use to look at God and say, "Where are You? I don't want to do these drugs. I don't want to take sixty laxatives a day so I can be little. I don't want to throw up twelve times a day. I don't want to do that. I want to eat my food and keep it down."

I would remember what my mother said to me when I was younger: "You're fat and I don't want to take you shopping." I would go in the store and hide under the clothes.

My mother would say, "Zona, where are you?" I wouldn't answer, but would continue hiding under the clothes. I thought, *If I lose weight, maybe she will love me. Maybe she'll think that I'm not a mistake.* So I got this preconceived idea it all had to do with the way I looked.

When we speak of God's love, we must never think of it in terms of any type of human love. The two are not even related. You see, God *is* love. He does not have love; He *is* love. Human love can be aroused and is open to manipulation. God's love, however, does not become excited by outside influences. He loves because He *is* love. God's love never fails. His love for you is not an emotion that is aroused by your beauty, your behavior or your morality.

God does not love you because you are a spiritually beautiful person. Neither is His love withheld because you are wretched and miserable. God loves you because of who He is, not because of who we are. His love cannot be earned, nor is it for sale. We can't manipulate His love by our behavior or circumstances. His love arises from within Himself.

He loved us before we were born. He loved us before we had any track record to place before Him. His love can only be received with wonder and grateful thanks. When we try to earn His love, we actually push ourselves away from Him because His love arises from who He is. His love is a gift offered without merit. It's always freely and unconditionally bestowed upon you.

Why does the sun shine on a lake as it goes down at night? Is it because the lake has somehow earned the right to reflect the sun so beautifully? No, the sun shines on the lake because the lake is there. The sun on the lake warms the waters. The waters sparkle and become radiant because the sun first shines on them. Apart from the sun, the lake would be cold and dark.

God is limitless, which means His love is limitless. He loves each of us as though we were the only ones created. That's how He loves each of us. Nobody has your face. Nobody has your voice. You are your own individual person and you have His undivided attention. You are the object of His concern. God knows what's going on with you.

Every time you call on His name, it is as though you alone have His attention. Do you get this? You're never out of His thoughts! I don't care how many devils try to come against you, you are still not out of His thoughts. He loves you. You can never do anything so bad that He will not love you—nothing at all.

We're not out of His thoughts for even a pepper-speck of a second. Whether we're asleep or awake, successful or a failure, whether we tell the truth or lie, whether we're a pervert or perfect - it doesn't matter. His love is unconditional toward you. Some people may have a perverted mind, but God still loves them. You may cuss like a sailor, but God still loves you. God is unchangeable and His love is as predictable as He is. His love toward us will never warm or cool – it is unchageable!

He will never run low on His supply of love. He will never love us more than He does at this moment. He will never become bored and leave us for a new or more exciting lover. All His love is now and forever the same - yesterday, today and forever. We were created to live in the consciousness of God's unconditional love for us.

Years ago when I used to think that nobody loved me, I didn't think that my dad loved me because he had all the businesses to consume his attention. Before he gave his heart to the Lord, it was like I would say, "I love you Dad!" and he would say, "Well, here's a twenty dollar bill. Go and buy yourself something." He had so many businesses. He had seven restaurants at one time and he owned a manufacturing company in another state. He had forty-two salesmen who went across the states to the universities, colleges, fraternities and sororities. They sold sportswear, stationary, envelopes, invitations, and graduation supplies. Besides that, he owned an auto auction where he sold cars.

When I was a teenager, Dad also owned property, divided lots, and built homes. He bought a hotel and a Jewish synagogue in Daytona.

But after that, when he gave his heart to the Lord, he went into the ministry. Then he was just as busy with the Full Gospel Business Men, Faith Memorial Church, winning young people to the Lord, and bringing in speakers like Brother Kenneth Hagin, Lester Sumrall, and John Osteen. He brought in Nicky Cruz, David Wilkerson and many other people who went to the high schools in Chattanooga, Benton, and Cleveland.

My dad was a busy man. When I started living with him, I would stay by myself a lot. I had to be a good girl. I never sneaked out, and I never had anybody in the house. I was kind of scared.

One night, my dad came home at midnight. My aunt was there, checking on me. She came by the house, looked in the window and saw that I was in the apartment. I was watching the television, lying on the couch with a water gun in my hand. My dad drove by, saw her there and just kept going because he knew the wrath of my aunt was about to come down.

You have to understand something. I didn't think that anybody loved me. I felt like I was rejected. Everything else was put first—ministry, God, and everything else. That's why I turned against everything. You can understand that.

Then when my dad came back to the Lord—really gave His heart to God, and started serving Him - the Lord said to him, "The thing you want the most in the world (Zona's salvation) won't happen until you understand one thing. When she comes in at 2:00 or 3:00 in the morning, do not scream at her. Only tell her, 'I love you' and then shut up, because she doesn't believe that anyone loves her."

Because my dad obeyed this word from God, I finally found out what the love of God truly meant. Dad had to get knowledge of the Word of God and then act in obedience to what God said so that I could know the true nature of the love of God. You can find out who God is by worshipping Him, but also, you have to study His ministry.

Only then will you know the true nature of the love of God and know how to share that love with others.

You see, we were created to be loved by God and we can't function apart from that love. If you're separated from God, loneliness will cause you to spend your days searching for a substitute love that's big enough to satisfy the void that was specially made for God's presence in your life.

I believe in telling young people the truth. If they don't understand the love of God, they won't get anywhere. When we're in close relationship with people, we can see the emptiness in their innermost core that cries out for a relationship with God. All these people with whom you are associating have been placed in your path for a reason. You have to love them with the love of God.

You have to love people with the love of God, without expecting anything from them in return. Just love them because of who they are. Don't love a person because of what you think they can do for you; love them for who they are. There is no person who can do anything for you that God can't do. Put all your trust and expectation in God and not in anything or anybody else. If you do trust in others, you will be let down every time.

An earthly marriage is a picture of what an ultimate relationship with God can be like. However, some people go through life changing their marriages like they change underwear. They are trying to find the perfect lover. What they don't realize is that the only God's love is perfect. To perfectly love others, you must love them with the love of God. That's exactly what my dad did. I needed to be loved right then because I felt that I never had love.

I needed somebody to love me regardless of how I acted. I needed someone to love me with God's love and not tell me of all the wrong things I had done. Love is not telling your daughter, "You're a disgrace. I can't believe you acted like that. You're straight from the pits of hell.

I would rather not be your dad." My dad would call me into his room and say, "I love you Zona and Jesus loves you." To this I would remark, "Are you finished?"

Maybe you think I responded that way because I was raised around money or was spoiled. That could not be further from the truth. I started working when I was fifteen years old. I always worked and never freeloaded off my dad. I borrowed money from my dad to start my fitness center, but made sure I repaid every debt. If I didn't pay on time, Dad's secretary would call me and say, "Your rent is past due." But now here was my dad loving me with the unconditional love of God. The love he showed me drew me toward God.

God wants you to get to know Him, to worship and not spend all your time working to earn His love. It's not a law that you have to worship Him. You're not going to go to hell if you don't worship God. God wants us to worship Him because He knows we will receive so many benefits when we worship Him. We can have God's benefits in our life. We can be living a free life, free from the devil, and free from any mind games. Experiencing God's love frees us to be a friend to someone else. That's one of the main things I see with Christian people today. They don't know how to be true friends because they don't know what the love of God really is.

No matter what, you have to totally love people where they're at. You can't receive and operate in the things of God unless you walk in the true love of God. You can't walk in the gifts or fruit of the Spirit unless you walk in the true love of God.

I had such a hard heart and my dad once had a hard heart. But all the time spent laying on the carpet of Faith Memorial Church and praying allowed God to melt that temper out of my dad. It went out of him just like it went out the window. It melted and he was never the same man. Now, my dad teaches me every day what the love of God truly is. He has so much of the love of God in Him. We just have to love people.

If you'll just let the true love of God come into you, it won't matter what else happens in your life. When the growths came off of me, I didn't feel anything. It was like a normal day when I got out of school. I went in that day and Sister Hagin taught me how to separate my clothes for winter, spring, summer, and fall. I was cleaning out my closet and I didn't feel anything. I looked at my hands—warty as everything with all those growths all over the place. I looked at my hands all the time. I reached up to get my dresses and looked at my hands with disgust and frustration. I just wanted the growths to be cut off.

I put the dresses down and then reached back up again. At that moment, I saw that all the growths were GONE. I ran to my dad and looked at him and said, "Dad, I don't even do anything for God—nothing! I don't even want anybody to know that I'm a Christian because I want to be cool in school. I don't even let anybody know that I go to church. Dad, I live a double life. You mean that God loves me so much that He took those growths off my body?"

I hugged my dad; he hugged me and I cried and cried and cried. My dad cried. The presence of God came in there and went from the top of our heads, spreading like warm honey all the way down to the soles of our feet. But I wasn't yet ready to serve God.

One night, as I was in the prime of my rebellion, I got on my knees. I was on drugs and I was trying to get off them. I was going to bed and my heart was beating ninety miles an hour every night. I got down on my knees and said, "I don't even know if You're real. I don't even know if You're listening to me, but I've got to have help or I'm going to die. You've got to help me. I am just asking You to help me. I don't want to take these drugs. I do not want to take this speed. I just do not want to take it."

The change didn't happen overnight. I went from taking twelve pills to taking ten. Another month went by and I went down to nine, but eventually, I got totally off the drugs. From the time I was a senior in high school, for twelve and a half years, I would go in the bathroom and I would see myself with rolls of fat, even though I only weighed 110 pounds. I would go eat, stick my finger down my throat, and I would throw up.

Then I got on the laxative thing. I took sixty laxatives a day. I would go in the store and steal them. I was messed up and thought, *Am I just messed up? What is wrong with me? Can I not just be normal?* In the midst of all of this, God still loved me. I worked the book table for my dad and I had the best sales records of anyone. All the while, I had two tablets of speed in the billfold of my purse. Nobody knew it but me.

After two years of living this lie, I finally walked in the bathroom and threw the speed down the commode. In all of this, God still loved me. He blessed me as I sold books and tapes.

We can't fathom the love of God. It will get rid of any demon. It will get rid of cancer. It will get rid of a confused mind. It will make the rebellious return. I know that. But first, you have to get a revelation of the love of God, of what He did on the cross and beyond the cross. You have to get it.

If you are stirred in your heart while reading this book, I encourage you to make an altar where you are at and surrender to God. Nobody can surrender for you. You have to do it yourself. Get on your knees and ask God to fill you with the love of God. It is all about you and God!

# CHAPTER 2

## PERSONAL REVELATION
## OF THE FATHER'S LOVE

*"Then said Jesus unto his disciples, If any man will come after me,
let him deny himself, and take up his cross, and follow me. For
whosoever will save his life shall lose it: and whosoever will lose his
life for my sake shall find it. For what is a man profited, if he shall
gain the whole world, and lose his own soul?*
*or what shall a man give in exchange for his soul?"*

*Matthew 16:24-26*

When church leadership is willing to change and they come
together in unity and want change in themselves, the devil hates
it. We need to take very seriously what the Bible says. In this passage
from Matthew, Jesus is telling His disciples to deny themselves. He
is saying the same thing to us today. If any man or woman will come
after me, Jesus says, let him deny himself. You see, it's not all about
what you want or who's right or wrong. Jesus is telling us we must deny
ourselves and take up our crosses and follow Him.

He goes on to say that whosoever will save his life shall lose it.
We are so interested in our own well being today, in making sure that
everyone thinks we are right and righteous. We need to be worried
about sin in our own lives first—not be trying to sweep off everybody
else's porch. We need to make sure our porch is clean. Everybody's got
an opinion, but the only opinion that matters is God's opinion. We
must make sure we are clean in His sight. What the Word says is what
matters. You have to be grounded and rooted in the Word, measuring
your life by what is written in God's Word. It doesn't matter what

some other teacher or preacher says, you have to be grounded and rooted in the Word.

The passage goes on to say, "… and whosoever will lose his life for my sake shall find it. For what is a man profited, if he gain the whole world, and lose his own soul?" (Matthew 16:25-26, KJV). If you don't stay in the Word and get grounded and rooted in the ministry of Jesus, you're going to lose your soul. Do not underestimate the importance of the personal relationship between you and Jesus. It's a very serious matter when you ask Jesus to be your personal Lord and Savior. I don't care if you have 5,000 notes in your Bible written in 10,000 colors, none of that matters. That doesn't make you more spiritual than anybody else. What matters is whether or not you have a personal relationship with Jesus.

I don't care how loudly you yell at the altar. I don't care if you're crying. It doesn't matter how spiritual you try to get yourself to look. If these things are all you're concerned about, you'll lose your own soul. Your chief concern must be whether or not you are in a relationship with Jesus Christ. That's most important – how it is between you and Him.

"For what is a man profited, if he should gain the whole world, and lose his own soul? Or what shall a man give in exchange for his soul" (Matthew 16:26, KJV)? Is there anything more important than the condition of your soul? What people think of you doesn't matter. How you look in the eyes of others doesn't matter. What matters is the condition of your soul, and the condition of your soul is determined by the status of your personal relationship with Jesus Christ.

You are responsible for what God tells you to do—not me. You're going to have to answer for what God tells you to do. Your value is not based in what people think about you, because other people's opinions are going to change from day to day. What matters is what God says about you and God says, "You're the best thing I've got."

The mind of a Pharisee thinks truth and perfect performance is more important than love, but Jesus showed us that love is the most important part. You can make mistake after mistake, after mistake, after mistake, after mistake, and God will not ever change His mind about you. He still values you, still loves you, and still wants a personal relationship with you. If only we could get that through to some of the religious people, that would be fine!

It seems to me that there are a lot of people who don't understand the love of God. They want to judge people by every single thing they say and do. Because that is their mindset, they don't know how to live loved. The love of God has meaning only if you can learn how to live loved. It only has meaning if you, as an individual, can learn to wake up every morning, confident that the Father delights over you every day. He truly does delight over you.

It doesn't matter if you committed fornication the night before, if you committed adultery the night before, or if you got drunk the night before. None of that matters; He delights over you. I don't mark people. That's the problem with the human race; they want to mark people for being rotten. I just don't mark people and neither does God. He loves you regardless of what you have or have not done.

I would never have come back to the Lord if it hadn't been for my daddy paying the price. He put up with so much from me, and yet he paid the price to love me. He did this because God spoke to him and told him to tell me that he loved me and that God loved me. God knew that I didn't believe anybody loved me. Now if love doesn't mean that much to the Lord, then why did He say that to my dad?

When my dad heard from the Lord, he said, "What do you mean? I love my daughter."

God replied, "The thing that you want the most in the world (for me to return to the Lord) will never happen. She's gone too far out in darkness; she can't hear me." God knew that the only thing that would get through to me was love, so that's what He told my dad to show me. And he did.

I had never lived loved. I had to work through that and I didn't get free of that until a few years ago. But what started the process rolling was my dad obeying God and showing me the unconditional, personal love of God.

I've spent many years trying to measure the width and depth of God's love, but it has been very hard for me to do so. I didn't see the love of God in a lot of people throughout my life. I didn't see the example of God's love from others until much later in my life. Now, every day I keep discovering more and more how incredible God is and how freely I can live when I am confident in Him. This is the only way you're going to get free from offense or anything that anybody does or says to you.

People take offense because they don't know the love of God. Every day I discover something new about God and how He wants to live in me. When I read the Word, it's like I read it with eyes of love, even if the Word is reprimanding me. If you're easily offended, you're not very spiritual. Always remember, if you get offended easily, it's an indication that you're not grounded and rooted in the Word. You're grounded and rooted in knowledge. You may know the Word, but you don't have it in your heart. The Word has got to be in your heart. A heart full of the Word is a soft heart, where each verse can be planted like a seed.

Recently, I was telling someone that living in God's love is difficult for so many because they think it's too complex, but it's actually very simple to live in His love. It's so simple. Don't assume that you can live this life out of intellect and your emotions. Time after time when I talk to people over the phone, I can say something about God and they say, "Well, I can't even believe you said that."

I reply, "Why not? That's what the Word says. I'm just telling it to you in plain English."

They'll ask, "Well, what verse is that?" I'll read them the verse and then I'll tell it to them in plain English and they'll say, "Oh, oh, I got it. I got it! You mean, I have to be confident basically in who I am in Christ Jesus and get rid of sowing into myself and living for myself and learn to live in Him?"

I then tell them, "Yeah! It's as simple as that!"

Your intellect and emotions are a very important part of your journey in this life, but nothing is more important than receiving a personal revelation of the Father's love. For years, I've talked to people about how much Jesus loves them. I've tried to describe His love with words, but words don't mean anything until you get the revelation of what God's love is to you. I can't make it happen for you. I'm not going to even try because I don't want to waste your time.

To get a revelation of God's love, ask Him to show you the depth of His love for you and the revelation of what the cross of Jesus accomplished. He seems to love doing this more and more for me. I was telling a minister, "I can be walking down the mall and all of sudden, I can see Jesus walking with a cross on His back. I'll see the Roman soldiers nailing Him to the cross. It's like I'm there with the woman who had an issue of blood or blind Bartimaeus when they had their encounters with Jesus. It's like I'm there." God's Word must become that real to us.

If you came into a room where a two-year-old child was playing and you wanted to have a relationship with that child, what would you have to do to make that happen?

That little child is a smart cookie. She knows when someone is genuine and when someone is not. She will respond to genuine love.

That's how it is with the Lord. If you're hungry for a relationship with Him, He will show you genuine love to draw you in personally. He'll take the initiative, but you have to invite him. Just ask Him to reveal Himself and show you how much He loves you.

# CHAPTER 3

## DOORWAYS TO DIVISION

*"Now I beseech you, brethren, mark them which cause divisions and offenses contrary to the doctrine which ye have learned; and avoid them"*

*Romans 16:17*

When you're doing what is right, you will have persecution and there will be an onslaught of attacks against your church. The devil will try to divide your church, for that is his work. God's love, however, unifies the body of Christ. To walk in unity in the love of God, we need to know the doorways to division so we can avoid them.

When there is an undercurrent of division in the church, the pastor has to address it as soon as possible. The pastor needs to share the church's statement of faith with the people and clarify what the church believes the Word says. This will help keep others from developing their own doctrine and is an important tool to keep peace and unity in the church.

It is important that the church work together in the unity of God's love. When people are not unified, when they are scattered, they are like sheep with no shepherd. "Then Micaiah told him, "In a vision I saw all Israel scattered on the mountains, like sheep without a shepherd'" (1 Kings 22:17, NLT). It is the job of the pastor to lead the fight in keeping unity in the church through the love of God.

I've seen the importance of a church being fitly joined together, as God called them to be. I've also seen the lengths to which Satan will go to divide a congregation. I want to show you five divisive influences the Lord has spoken about, which I have observed over the years. If these influences are left in a church or allowed to operate unhindered in your life, they'll open the door to division.

Please note, I am bringing this message with a pure heart. I have no ulterior motives or hidden agendas. My desire truly is to train people so that they can avoid Satan's schemes.

# #1 - A Hireling or Wolf Pastor Causes Division

You have to understand that the number one dividing factor in a church can be the pastor, if he is a hireling or a wolf. The pastor has a major role to play in building a strong core in the body of Christ. If a pastor doesn't embrace that role and seek to fulfill it, there will be division in the church. A pastor has to be strong enough where he can't be swayed. No matter what anybody says or what his neighbor might be preaching or teaching, if a pastor can stay strong in the Word, he will be able to stand in this hour. If your pastor doesn't feed you with the Word, then you need to go to church somewhere else.

Consider these words of Jesus: "I am the good shepherd: the good shepherd giveth his life for the sheep. But he that is a hireling, and not the shepherd, whose own the sheep are not, seeth the wolf coming, and leaveth the sheep, and fleeth: and the wolf catcheth them, and scattereth the sheep. The hireling fleeth, because he is a hireling, and careth not for the sheep. I am the good shepherd, and know my sheep, and am known of mine" (John 10:11-14, KJV).

Now, from a biblical standpoint, Jesus Christ is the chief Shepherd and local pastors, such as me, are the under-shepherds. In fact, the Greek word translated "shepherd" in this passage from John 10 is also often translated "pastor." Now that tells us some things about the office of a pastor. Keeping this in mind, we have a new understanding of the role of the pastor in the church.

There are three key words in this passage that you must note and understand. The first word is *wolf.* Without fail in the New Testament, this word refers to a person who is being used of the devil to promote division in the body of Christ, sometimes without them even knowing they're being used. These people may love God and not intend any harm, but they are spiritual children who haven't grown up in the faith and they simply don't know any better than to do what they're doing.

The next word is *scattereth.* The person acting as a wolf always has the effect of scattering the sheep. The spirit to which the wolf has yielded creates division in the church. A church divided, scatters.

The last word is *hireling.* The Lord is telling us that it's possible for a person to stand in the office of pastor who isn't truly called and appointed by God. A hireling is a pastor who is hired by a board, the deacons or some other committee, rather than being appointed and anointed by God to fulfill a calling. Hirelings have no God-given ability to maintain unity and prevent turmoil.

Now please do not misunderstand. Just because drama breaks out in your ministry, doesn't automatically mean that the pastor is not called to fulfill the office of a pastor. If drama breaks out, the pastor needs to deal with the situation by boldly confronting it. When a person stands in the office of pastor, they carry an anointing from God. Their job is to keep the wolf away. They keep division away by standing strongly in their anointing, sure of their call as they contend for the sake of the church.

If a pastor is not called and anointed by God for that office, he will either be unable or unwilling to fulfill this important duty. If there is no pastoral anointing, there is no one to keep the wolf away from the flock. This will result in people becoming isolated from the body of Christ and devoured by the devil.

Now, there are other cases in which people choose not to be connected to the flock. Why would people allow themselves to be cut off from their church? I can think of only a few reasons why individuals wouldn't stay under the covering of a pastor. The first reason is simply that they've neglected to be committed to a local church. Church hoppers don't know that God sends every member to a local body as it pleases Him and that is why they hop around from one meeting to another. They don't know that God has a specific place for them to receive what they need. The Bible says that the sheep know the voice of their shepherd. When you're in a church where God called you to be, you're going to recognize the voice of the shepherd as God's voice coming from the pulpit.

The second reason why an individual wouldn't stay under the covering of a pastor is because there is a hireling in the pulpit. There are two ways to find out if a pastor is a hireling. The first way is to listen to the way the pastor preaches or teaches. Is there authority in her message? Secondly, look for the fruit of her ministry. If the anointing is there, you'll see the fruit of her ministry come forth. There will be no lack.

Look around your church. Are people are being blessed of the Lord? Are people receiving their healing, getting their miracles, and learning how to stand on their own in the Word? You have to judge a tree by the fruit. If there's no good fruit, then the pastor is a hireling.

The last reason why people may choose to stand outside the pastor's covering may be less apparent. The fact is that the ministry of a pastor must be received by faith if a person is to benefit from the anointing that flows through the pastor. "And we beseech you, brethren, to know them which labor among you, and are over you in the Lord, and admonish you; and to esteem them very highly in love for their work's sake. And be at peace among yourselves" (I Thessalonians. 5:12-13 KJV).

You see, it's the office of pastor that you need to esteem highly, and not the person who stands in the office. Your faith needs to be in the anointing that resides in and on the office—not in the talent of the man who stands behind it.

In my church, when Pastor Craig leads praise and worship, I receive so much from him because I know how pure he is inside and how sure the anointing and call of God is upon his life. People often allow the personality of a man to get in the way of the anointing. They are irritated by the man's mannerisms, accent, or something about his flesh. They say, "Well, he just doesn't hit me quite right!" They need to look beyond the man and see Jesus. He's the author and finisher of our faith. Having this attitude starts with walking in God's love.

So every time you sit under a pastor's teaching, believe that God will speak through him into your life and then you'll be spiritually fed. Have a spirit of expectation. If you'll draw on the anointing by faith, you will keep the wolf of division out of your life!

Before I leave this subject, I want to share one more verse with you. "And I will set up shepherds over them which shall feed them: and they shall fear no more, nor be dismayed, neither shall they be lacking, saith the Lord" (Jeremiah 23:4, KJV).

Some people say, "I can't receive from that teacher or preacher because of this or that." But the truth is, when you sit under the ministry of a pastor, you can believe God to feed you. Your life can be an adventure in God and you can expect no lack of any kind in your life. Expect no lack of love, no lack of peace, no lack of joy, no lack of anything. You will experience victory if you'll just open the Word, read it, renew your mind, build up yourself in the Holy Ghost and live in the love of God.

## #2 - Spiritual Manifestations Cause Division

The second thing that causes division in a church is hunger for supernatural manifestations. "Beware of false prophets, which come to you in sheep's clothing, but inwardly they are ravening wolves" (Matthew 7:15, KJV).

In this scripture, the word *prophet* means one who proclaims God's Word. It doesn't necessarily refer to the office of a prophet, but rather to somebody who preaches and teaches the Word of God. False prophets are ravening wolves who divide the flock, and they come in sheep's clothing. They don't look like devils. They don't look like bad people. They do good and they look sound, but inwardly they have a divisive influence on the body of Christ.

How can you tell if somebody is a ravening wolf? You will know them by their fruit (Matthew 7:16). What kind of fruit does a wolf produce? A wolf scatters and divides. "Many will say to me in that day, Lord, Lord, have we not prophesied in thy name? and in thy name have cast out devils? and in thy name done many wonderful works? And then will I profess unto them, I never knew you: depart from me, ye that work iniquity" (Mathew 7:22-23, KJV).

Some say, "I don't get it Zona. How can prophesying, casting out devils, and doing wonderful works be iniquity?" They aren't. The iniquity is the division that the wolf brings under the covering of spiritual manifestations. Spiritual manifestations are not the measure of a valid ministry. If that is what you hunger for, then the devil will surely accommodate you.

Many people go to a meeting somewhere and get "loud" because of the spiritual manifestations. Then when they return to their old church, they suddenly feel frustrated and dissatisfied because they aren't seeing those same manifestations in the services. Following the wolf's manifestations, they can be drawn away from God's will in going to a particular church or Bible School. That's happened to many. They become isolated from their designed part in the body of Christ.

Please don't misunderstand what I'm saying. It's good to hunger for more of God's power and presence. Paul instructs us that we should covet earnestly the best gifts, but that desire has to be built on a solid foundation, and that's the Word of God (1 Corinthians 12:31, KJV).

There are to be no performances in the church of God. He is to be the basis of everything. That's what my dad, Brother Hagin, Brother Osteen, and Brother Sumrall taught me. Jesus also tells us how to avoid this kind of division: "Therefore whoever hears these sayings of Mine, and does them, I will liken him to a wise man who built his house on the rock" (Matthew 7:24, NKJV). Jesus is saying if you don't want to get drawn away by the supernatural manifestations of a ravening wolf, build your search for God's power upon the foundation of My words.

Don't try to dissect the Word; just take it for what it is. It's simple. A valid ministry is built only on the Word of God. Supernatural manifestations are awesome, but if you rely on them, you'll get in trouble. Your greatest hunger for the things of God has to be based on the Word of God. Then you can flow with the supernatural without the danger of being led astray.

## #3 - Itching Ears Cause Division

The third thing that causes division in a church is people with itching ears. Paul exhorts Timothy, "Preach the word; be instant in season, out of season; reprove, rebuke, exhort with all long suffering and doctrine" (2 Timothy 4:2, KJV). Paul is telling Timothy to preach the whole counsel of the Word. At our church, we teach the whole Word of God and not just the portions of the Word that deal with worship, faith, or devils. The whole Word works together. We don't just teach the parts of the Word that people want to hear.

But Paul does not stop there in his message to Timothy. In verse 3, he tells Timothy - and us - why people need to hear the whole Word: "For the time is coming when [people] will not tolerate (endure) sound and wholesome instruction, but, having ears itching [for something pleasing and gratifying], they will gather to themselves one teacher after another to a considerable number, chosen to satisfy their own liking and to foster the errors they hold" (II Timothy 4:2-3, AMP).

We all have favorite teachings from God's Word, but it's dangerous to just stick to one topic. Some prefer to study the promises concerning healing. Others prefer portions concerning the covenant of increase. Another prefers teachings on grace; another is interested in scriptures on demons. Still another might want to focus on how to walk in the fruit of the Spirit. Some people get stuck on the topic of the end times. Whatever your favorite part, you must not let your desire to focus on a particular part of the Word keep you from studying all the other parts. No matter how important it might be to you, you must put yourself in a church where you can hear all the Word of God.

Some people get stuck on one topic and they won't hear anything else. We must not get off on tangents. If you're not happy with the Word that's being preached at the church where God sent you, then your ears are beginning to itch. If you scratch that itch by going somewhere else where you can hear more of what you want to hear instead of accepting teachings from the full Bible, then you can count on your heart being deceived and damaged.

There are plenty of churches that will look to find a scripture to accommodate your flesh if you leave yourself wide open for deception. Don't allow yourself to be drawn away from the place where God sent you. God has sent you to that place because He loves you and wants to give you His very best. Accept the love of God that is extended to you through the teachings of His messenger.

## #4 - Offense Causes Division

The fourth thing that causes division in a church is people who allow themselves to be offended. Offense is probably the most common cause for people to be separated from the church where God has called them. They become offended at the church or at an individual in the church.

You know, you do have a choice whether or not to be offended. "And herein do I exercise myself, to have always a conscience void of offense toward God, and toward men" (Acts 24:16, KJV). You can exercise your will and never allow yourself feel justified in being offended, but this requires great strength. You have to be solid in your thinking. You must understand just how devilish offenses are and make a decision not to be offended at anybody, no matter what. You have to make up your mind.

I come across some people who are offended by the most ridiculous things I ever heard in my life. Once, a person got upset and didn't come back to church because we paved the parking lot and while the work was being done, we blocked the parking lot off with chains. They thought we were kicking them out. People who get offended say, "I couldn't get an appointment with Pastor Zona as quickly as I wanted. She was talking to me from the pulpit. I know she was talking to me because she was looking right at me, and she was pointing her finger at me." I hear those types of things all the time.

I'm charged by God to preach the uncompromised Word in such a way as to leave you with no wiggle room at all. I'm not going to sneak around the truth. My commission to the pastoral office does not allow me to sneak around the truth – but don't take it personally. The other day I said something about being "stupid" in my message and later I thought, *Oh Lord, I hope nobody took that comment the wrong way.* Then I thought to myself, *My dad can get away with that, but then again, he's eighty-five years old. He can pretty much get away with anything. He's paid the price to be able to do that, more than you have, Zona.*

You see, if you become offended at your pastor, then you're in danger of being cut off from any type of anointing that passes through that preacher and you distance yourself from the love of God. You have to accept the message the minister has been given by God to deliver.

Any tendency to become offended is actually rooted in pride. That's why offense is so dangerous. Instead of getting offended, deal with the pride that causes the offense and whatever you do, keep the door of division closed.

# #5 – YOU May Cause Division

The fifth thing that causes division in a church is oftentimes the people. "Now I beseech you, brethren, mark them which cause divisions and offenses contrary to the doctrine which ye have learned; and avoid them" (Roman 16:17, KJV).

Let me be blunt with you for just a moment. Are you causing division and offenses in the church? Let me ask you another question. Have you allowed yourself to be used by the devil to try to divide the body of Christ? If you have, that's bad for your fellow church members, but it's much worse for the person who has been instrumental in causing the division.

The most miserable, unhappy Christians I know are those who unknowingly fall into the trap of being used by the devil to divide churches. I saw these situations in every church I attended when I was growing up. I have seen it in church after church as an adult. My dad was telling me about a certain church that was once a thriving church that has now been reduced to eighteen people because of divisions.

How can you tell if you are causing division and what can you do about it if you are? The greatest indicator that Satan may try to use you to cause division is if you tend to be critical, finding fault with everything. Do you tend to see the negative side of everything? That is a warning sign of a divisive personality. People who have critical spirits will never offer constructive solutions to problems. They just try to find fault.

The truth is that no person is immune from this disease. We've all been critical. I guess the reason I haven't been too critical in my life is because I've had to fight for my life so much. I remember when I was on dialysis the first time. I was just talking ninety miles an hour inside my spirit, and God said to me, "The word 'listen' and the word 'silent' have the same letters." When I heard that, I knew God was telling me to be quiet and listen to Him, rather than speak critically about others or about my situation. We all tend to do that—criticize other people or situations.

People with critical spirits don't offer any constructive solutions to the problem. They don't have anything to offer but criticism. A critical spirit is a disease. Criticism is a habit that has to be broken. Mature people don't get offended. If you find it easier to speak negative reports instead of exhorting and promoting the positive, ask the Lord to make a change in you. That's what I do all the time. I try to keep myself in check.

The grace message must be heard with your spiritual ears. You cannot listen to the grace message with your natural ears. You have to be mature enough and listen to it with your spiritual ears. You have to ask God for the ability to see people with the compassion of Jesus. That's what I do every day of my life. I ask God to give me His ideas that will promote His Word in the church.

Once when I prayed this prayer, for three weeks God kept saying to me, "Address the division thing. Address the division thing. Address the division." I said, "I don't want to, I don't want to. I don't want to." But after three weeks, I wanted to address the division issue. I don't want to be in disobedience. There may not be any major issues God wants you to address, but whatever it is that may be working to cause division, you have to nip it in the bud.

We have to promote unity in the church. We have to be of the same mind. "Now I beseech you, brethren, by the name of our Lord Jesus Christ, that ye all speak the same thing, and that there be no divisions among you; but that ye be perfectly joined together in the same mind and in the same judgment" (1 Corinthians 1:10, KJV). Unity will release the corporate anointing in a church and change a city. If one can put a thousand to flight, and two can put ten thousand to flight, what can ten thousand who are joined together in unity do? When we're all perfectly joined together in the same mind, in one accord without division, then the power of God will fall. Then we'll all realize the purpose of God in our lives—corporately and individually.

Unfortunately today, everybody is in everybody's business and then they try to get me in your business. I don't need to know your business. God is the only one who needs to know your business. We've got to quit looking for the worst in people. This is an issue of the heart – a lack of love for others and lack of love for God. We need to get an understanding of God's love. Look at what the Bible says, "May Christ through your faith [actually] dwell (settle down, abide, make His permanent home) in your hearts! May you be rooted deep in love and founded securely on love, that you may have the power and be strong to apprehend and grasp with all the saints [God's devoted people, the experience of that love] what is the breadth and length and height and depth [of it]; [that you may really come] to know [practically, through experience for yourselves] the love of Christ, which far surpasses mere knowledge [without experience]; that you may be filled [through all your being] unto all the fullness of God [may have the richest measure of the divine Presence, and become a body wholly filled and flooded with God Himself]! Now to Him Who, by (in consequence of) the [action of His] power that is at work within us, is able to [carry out His purpose and] do superabundantly, far over and above all that we [dare] ask or think [infinitely beyond our highest prayers, desires, thoughts, hopes, or dreams]— to Him be glory in the church and in Christ Jesus throughout all generations forever and ever. Amen (so be it)" (Ephesians 3:17-21, AMP).

So many things vie for a place in our heart. What's in your heart? God, Jesus, and the Holy Spirit? Thoughts about finances, salvation, forgiveness, your past, prayers, marriage, and health? Righteousness, eternity, your weight, people's opinion of you, your children, fears about the economy, and God's opinion of you? Your dreams, your ability, your opinion of others, who you are, friendships, and success? Your spouse, desires, beauty, your family, trials, protection, future love, self-image, acceptance, and approval? All of those things are often found in your heart!

But the most important thing is that Christ, through your faith, actually dwells, settles down, abides, and makes His permanent home in your heart. It is imperative that you be rooted and founded securely in love. That is why the apostle Paul prayed that through your faith, Jesus would dwell and abide in your heart and you would be rooted deeply and secure in His love.

Your heart is your mind, thoughts, and emotions. It's where you decide what you believe, and the beliefs of your heart are established through what you've experienced in life and what you've been taught—even if those things were wrong. Sometimes we believe false things and honestly it's not really our fault. I was brought up to believe "once saved, always saved" all my life, but that's not what the Word teaches. It took me a long time to break that belief. When you have family that teaches you a way that's not in the Word, it's hard to break that belief! But the fact is, it's either in the Word or it's not in the Word and you can't manipulate, conjure up or do anything to make the Word fit what you want to believe.

To break out of a false belief, you must resist the devil, who would seek to lead you astray, and you've got to have faith in God's grace to get you out. Submit yourself to God and resist the devil. That's it—period! To get through life, you must have faith in grace. You can't just teach grace. You've got to have faith in grace. You have to be solid. You can't be led astray with every wind and doctrine.

Paul prayed that your heart would be centered in Christ and what He accomplished for you. He prayed that your mind, your thoughts and your emotions would be filled with the truth of who you are in Jesus and His great love for you. How more solid foundation can you get?

You can't get me to budge off the Word. There is no way. I don't care if I lost Terry, Lee, and everybody else in my life and I'm left here by myself, I'll preach to the pews. I'm not turning from God and what His Word says.

In every area of your life, you need to believe the truth that God says about you and not the lies of the devil. You're strong in your finances. You're strong in salvation. You're strong in forgiveness. You're strong in your prayers. You're strong in your marriage. You're strong in your health. You're going to Heaven. You're strong in righteousness.

So stop caring what people think about you. Believe God's opinion of you. Believe your children are saved. Don't let the economy bother you. Be strong in your belief that God's Word is true.

You have God's approval. You are accepted in the body of Christ. Let God's opinion of you shape your self-image. You're protected by God. You have a hope and a future. You're strong enough to get through trials. You're a success. You're strong in all your friendships. You're strong because of who you are in Christ Jesus— period. You cannot let any other areas bother you.

You've got to know who you are in Christ Jesus. Then you've got to act out of that knowledge to build up the body of Christ. That is the way to ensure that you won't be a source of division in the church. When you believe the truth that God says about you, it will bring forth glory in every area. If you truly believe that what God says about you is true, you're going to have self-control, you're going to be confident, and you're going to know who you are in Christ Jesus. He loves you— period!

I've been a Christian for a long time, but it wasn't until I was in my 30's that I truly began to experience the fullness of life that Jesus died to give me. It wasn't until the last two years that I truly realized how much He loves me. My heart always believed I was lacking—and that's exactly what I experienced. Growing up, I thought I had to work to prove myself and do this and that. I thought I had to have a 4.0 grade point average. If I fell short, I beat myself up thinking, *I can't believe I didn't make a 4.0.*

In the last two years, I've experienced a transformation. I've devoted my heart, mind, and thoughts to Jesus and don't worry about what anybody else thinks or says. I've begun to continually think on the truth of who I am in Him. My mind has started being filled with thoughts like, *Jesus I know You love me because You died to make me righteous in You. Thank You for surrounding me with favor as a shield. I know You love me Lord, because You have proven Your love to me. No matter what, I am abundantly blessed because of You. I know that You love me and I'm never quitting, Lord. I don't care what they say. I'll never stop. I'm never quitting.*

This is the key to what has happened: God's Word began to really penetrate my heart and my heart started changing. My sense of lack disappeared. And then what God said about me began to manifest. From two years ago to right now, I don't even look the same!

As you get your mind on Jesus, you're going to find that your heart becomes full of light. As I pray in the Holy Ghost, it is like Popeye and spinach - I get stronger and stronger. When I find myself tired and run down, I spend about 45 minutes praying in the Holy Ghost and I just pop right back up. It's like pumping yourself up in the Holy Ghost. You'll experience your heart being filled with the fullness of God.

Why can't you experience this every day? God has an amazing plan for your life, but you have to be aware of it. There's a fight going on for your heart in the spirit realm. You have to understand that the devil's plan for your heart and life is to steal, kill, and destroy, but Jesus' plan is that you enjoy life and have it in abundance.

Do you really believe God's Word to be true? If so, that belief will bring life to you. There are so many people in the body of Christ who have been hurt. They don't even know how to love people right. They don't even love themselves, so how can they love others? Love is what is lacking in the body of Christ. This message is for the whole body—every church in America. I notice that a lot in the body of Christ are sadly lacking in the area of love.

My dad was driving to a meeting in Georgia many years ago when the Lord said to him, "Son, My children are sadly lacking."

Dad replied, "What do You mean, Lord?"

The Lord said, "They don't love and worship Me enough. They can quote the Word. They can give their money and cast out devils, but they don't love and worship Me enough and neither do you."

My dad said, "What do You mean I don't love and worship You enough? I go here and I go there. I speak here. I set up meetings for Kenneth Hagin. I set up meetings for John Osteen and we have revivals. I'm one who brings all these teachers into the high schools. I'm doing this and I'm doing that."

The Lord said, "That's exactly right. You're busy, busy, busy. All I want you to do is love and worship Me, because as long as you do that, no other voice will you follow. Building up somebody else's ministry is not going to get you the abundant life and even building up your own ministry is not going to get you an abundant life. You have to build yourself up in Me. Worship Me! Worship Me! Worship Me!"

Don't be so worried about the devil all the time. Just keep your heart right. Don't worry about somebody else's business. Find God for yourself and keep your front porch cleaned off, instead of trying to clean off somebody else's front porch.

Look to God for your value and your answers, not others. I once went to services just to hear somebody prophesy in front of me. I knew this prophet of God and I used to call him all the day and say, "Well, do you see anything brother?"

One day, God said to me, "I'm going to sever that relationship on good terms. I don't want My people going to a man to get guidance. I don't like anyone putting idols before Me." I went to meetings because there were prophets there and I needed a word. I've done that, but it's so wrong. I was putting the word they would provide in front of God's Word.

I used to sleep with my Bible. Then God said to me, "What are you doing sleeping with your Bible? It won't do any good. You need to open it up, read it, and get it in your heart. You can go to hell sleeping with your Bible, but if you get My Word in your heart, you'll never reject Me. You'll go to Heaven if you get it in your heart." We must take the Word in, believe it, and by faith accept the love of God. That will ensure that we are not a source of division.

*It's Been Love All Along*

# CHAPTER 4

## LOVE CHANGES YOUR WAY
## OF THINKING

*"But those things which proceed out of the mouth*
*come forth from the heart; and they defile the man."*

*Matthew 15:18*

A person can never receive the love of God until they find their mental roots. Notice, I didn't say they need to get in touch with their mental demons; I said mental roots. Has anybody ever told you, "I've made up my mind; this is what I'm going to do"? I think all of us have made this statement at one time or another. We're certainly capable of making independent decisions and our independent decisions are usually based on old information that's been programmed in our minds.

You've got to discover the areas of your thinking that led to bad decisions in your life. It's not difficult to change those thoughts, but the change may not happen immediately. Changing your thinking does take time and it requires using the Word.

You can change any part of your life physically, mentally, spiritually, financially and socially. Any area of your life can be changed. The key is to first change your way of thinking. Decide what you'll think and then your thinking will determine what's going to happen in your life.

In college, I did a study of the subconscious mind. I read over a great deal of research done by psychologists and psychiatrists who work with behavioral change. The material I read was based in some truth, but psychiatry is just the world's interpretation of God's psychology. God's psychology is revealed in the Scriptures. The Bible shows us how our soul is related to our body and spirit. I enjoyed this study because I've been a people watcher all my life and I know that our subconscious mind has to be changed in order for our lives to be changed. The ways of thinking that we learned when we grew up are still affecting our decisions today. The exciting thing is that you can change what is stored in your subconscious, which in turn can affect the choices you make today.

Many of your decisions were preprogrammed years ago. In the areas of marriage, ministry, and life, so many of your decisions were predetermined when you were a teenager. While we are young, we have to program the Word in our minds so by the time we reach our early teens, we can make the right decisions.

Nowadays, teenagers are going through a lot more than what I ever did as a teenager. When I was a teenager, you could leave your door open, unlocked, and nobody would go into your house. It was nothing for me, at twelve years old, staying in an apartment by myself until 11:00 or 12:00 at night. I did it all the time. But now, the world is totally different. There is so much coming against teenagers, it is more important than ever for them to get the Word in their minds at an early age so they can made right decisions later.

If you talk to the average person, you'll find that it's extremely rare to find someone who is happy with their life nowadays. I've never seen a prisoner who is happy with their past. I've never seen somebody who's in and out of rehab or somebody who came out of the streets who is happy with their past. In the soup kitchen, none of those people are happy with their past.

You may say, "Well, the reason that my subconscious mind is the way it is, is because I was beaten, I was raped, and I lived a life around drugs." These people are not happy with their past because their subconscious minds are programmed with antisocial thinking, so they automatically move back in that kind of life and get caught in the same messes again and again and again.

Most people believe that if they had more money, they would be better off. That's simply not true. I've met people in this ministry. You can't give them more than fifty dollars, and even that's too much. I ask them all the time, "What do you want out of life? Do you find yourself moving farther and farther away from what you want, in spite of everything you do?" Their answer to these questions is directly related to whether or not they are living in the love of God.

Is there some hidden thought process preventing you from living in the love of God and enjoying life to the fullest? What are your mental roots? You see, the very first thing you must understand are your reflex thoughts. Most people understand they have muscles in their bodies. My degree is in nutrition and I love the study of the body, how it works, and how every muscle, organ, tendon and bone works. It just amazes me. Most people understand they have muscles in their body and that those muscles were created to react to stimuli without any conscious thinking.

Your lungs are part of your reflex system. It's an automatic reaction to breathe. You don't have to think about breathing. You don't have to tell yourself to breathe. Your heart is a reflex organ. It pumps blood through your body without you thinking about it. You're not thinking, *My heart's going—it's beating, it's beating, it's beating.* The heart does its work automatically. If you hit your leg below your kneecap, you'll see a muscle react. Your leg will jump. You don't have to tell your leg to do that. It automatically does that. It'll react even if you try to stop it.

Your thoughts have to operate like that. All the thoughts that are in our subconscious mind are called reflex thoughts and those thoughts are the ones that automatically trigger words. They trigger our behavior. They trigger the patterns in our life. They are thoughts you're not thinking for the first time.

Unfortunately, most of our lives are spent acting on reflex thoughts stored in our subconscious mind. That's why there's turmoil. I'm trying to help you understand where your behaviors come from. You don't do what you do because you're bad. You do what you do because your reflex thoughts are based in faulty thinking. You may think you are in charge of your own life, but in reality, you are not. You may think you are making independent decisions, but in reality, you're making reflex decisions.

God sends people to a Bible College. They initially decide they're going to attend it four years, but then they leave. I've seen this happen several times. I've seen a pattern. They're being driven by reflex thoughts. This doesn't mean that anybody is bad. They're thinking habits, but thinking habits – like physical habits – sometimes have to be broken for the good of the person..

These reflex thoughts have everything to do with a generational devil hanging over you from the past. This kind of thinking has to be broken. Nobody can break that kind of thinking off you, however. You have to break it off yourself. You can't depend on anybody to get you free. You have to get yourself free and stay free.

If you don't learn it to break these reflex thinking patterns, you're going to be codependent on people the rest of your life. Only you can keep yourself free. Nobody can do it for you. You have to learn to be strong. You have to learn to stand up to the devil and tell him he can't have you and can't direct your thinking. He can't have anything about you.

No one thinks smoking tobacco is beneficial. No one thinks smoking is harmless. Yet, many people still smoke in spite of the health hazards. Not to mention the horrible odor! It took a national campaign linking smoking with an increased risk of cancer to cause people to change the program in their subconscious mind and stop smoking.

"Smoking is actually pleasant," somebody said. Others say, "I have to smoke. No one's going to make me quit if I don't want to." The truth is, most people who smoke cigarettes don't even think about lighting the first cigarette in the morning. They just automatically grab a cigarette and light it without ever making a conscious decision. This is called a habit, not a devil. You see what I'm saying? They don't think about getting a cigarette out of the pack, lighting the match or sucking the smoke into their lungs and blowing it out. All of those things are simply reflex actions.

There's so many more examples of reflex actions in everyday life—drinking coffee, driving to and from work, washing dishes, washing clothes, or even exercising. I'm on the Gazelle every morning for thirty minutes. It's just an automatic thing. These things become habits rooted in the subconscious part of our mind.

You can be a positive person. Let's look at this from an accounting perspective. I am a numbers person, so let's look at this in terms of assets and liabilities. Let's add the assets and liabilities together to determine whether you have a positive or negative situation in your life. What we are trying to determine in the end is net worth. One hundred percent of the time, the reason people stop midstream and don't fulfill the call of God on their life is because they don't understand their true net worth. They have no idea.

The majority of people do not understand that it doesn't matter how much you may have missed it, how many times you may have fallen short, past mistakes do not ultimately determine your net worth. It doesn't matter how much you screamed and hollered in the past. I lived with a screamer. My daddy was a screamer before he was set free. We've all had negative things in our lives, but those negative things do not determine your net worth.

You can't do anything so bad that you will not to have a net worth. You can't say anything bad enough. I want you to take an honest mental inventory and find the balance between your assets and liabilities. Once you realize that your assets outweigh your liabilities, you'll experience a happy and productive life. If you don't come to this realization, then most likely, you'll experience problems in your life.

You need to know what's being fed into your memory. If you're constantly fed the message, "You need to do this, you need to do that. You're not good enough, you can't accomplish that. There's no way," you will be led off track. Don't let the devil get you off track with these kinds of messages. You need to know what's being fed into your mind by the people surrounding you. If people are constantly badgering you, making you feel guilty, making you feel unworthy because maybe you made a wrong decision but now you have changed and gone back to what God has called you to do, they are not very mature.

Renewing your mind involves changing your conscious thinking, but more importantly it involves changes in the spirit of your mind. Changes in your physical life are manifestations of the inward changes you have made. Focus on the inward changes. But be careful not to tell everybody about your inward thinking. Sometimes when everybody gets together, they talk too much. You can talk yourself into depression. You can talk yourself out of attending Bible School or church. Be careful about what comes out of your mouth and be careful about taking in what comes from the mouths of others.

Your mind is the controlling mechanism of your life. Always remember something. You can't learn something from someone who doesn't know anything. I want you to always remember that your mind is a computer that stores information and controls things that happen around you. It controls decisions. It controls choices in your family, business, finances, health, and in all you do. Your mind is a controlling machine. So to the degree your mind is renewed, you will begin to experience change, and then you'll enter into a renewed life.

If you continue to focus on outward change only, you're going to miss the most important changes that can possibly happen. For example people may think, "Well I gave up this, and I gave up that. I can't believe I did this, I can't believe I did that. I can't believe I moved here. I can't believe I'm going to this little school." They will focus on the outward changes they have made. Most of us deal with life's symptoms as we focus on outward things and look at circumstances.

The devil is in the killing business. Most of us deal only with life's symptoms as we focus on the outward things and look at circumstances. We spend our time so focused on symptoms, we don't get to the root cause of the problem. Whatever is stored in us - good or bad treasure - that is what you will bring forth each day.

What gets us off focus sometimes is our belief that everything is related to a devil. Everything is not spiritual. Now, I do believe that Christians today are tired of mediocrity, but being tired of it doesn't mean you know how to change it. You may be tired of mediocrity and simply express frustration. But being tired and frustrated will not produce any change.

When you begin to change the spirit of your mind, you will begin to change the kind of treasure that's inside of you. Jesus said that your heart contains your treasure. When you accept the love of God in your heart, you see whatever goal lies before you and though it may look like it's the most difficult goal to accomplish, you can accomplish it. When you begin to change your heart and accept the love of God in your heart, that thing you need to change will change.

But if you think a devil is oppressing you all the time and you focus on a devil constantly, there will be no treasure in your heart. Focusing on devils does not build treasure; the love of God in your heart builds treasure. For instance, you can want to see yourself free, but you'll never get free just from wanting it to be so. You may say, "Yes, I'm going to get free. As I get older I will get free." The reality is that as you get older, you mature and realize what an idiot you were back then. The change in your life doesn't have anything to do with God; you're just tired of making the same dumb mistakes so you changed. Is that not the truth?

You may claim, "Well, God set me free!" No, you decided to mature and work a job and quit drinking. It had nothing to do with anything spiritual. Maybe somebody stood in the gap for you, but you made a conscious decision to get out of that previous lifestyle. You are living in a natural world and in a natural body.

God is interceding for you—not anybody else. He's the One interceding for you and only His love can bring a change to your life. Why would you depend on somebody to prophesy to you? Why would you depend on somebody to deliver you? Why would you depend on somebody to speak prosperity words to you? Why would you depend on someone else? You already have that inside of you if the love of God is in your heart.

There's nothing wrong with going to a meeting, but don't go just so somebody will give you a word. All you need for every day of your life can be found in the treasure of your heart. It's like a bank account for life. You draw on that bank account to deal with your spouse. You make a withdrawal when you interact with friends or somebody around you. You make a withdrawal when you interact with people on your job.

Every day, all of us make a withdrawal from the treasure in our hearts. Your heart has to be full of the love of God for you to live successfully. Is the treasure in your heart negative? Then it will bring forth the currency of worry. It'll bring the currency of defeat. It'll bring the currency of low self-worth. If your treasure is not based in God's love, you'll bring negative currency out of your spirit. Then your life will be filled with fear, depression, anxiety, sleepless nights, frustration, rejection, and thoughts that everybody is talking bad about you.

This message is to build you up. I am tired of devils coming amongst God's people wreaking havoc. I want a pure church. I want a church that's strong. I want a church that loves the Lord, stands on the Word, and is not focused so much on the devil that they forget about the love of God.

If things around you are negative all the time and you're always having to deal with the underworld, that is a reflection of what you have stored away in your heart. If you're struggling financially, look around you. Prosperity is not just about money. Sometimes we can have a poverty mentality that affects everything we touch. You may have a poverty mentality where health or relationships are concerned. Every day you bring that mentality forth and experience it in your life. Think about what treasure is stored in your heart. If you've been divorced or you're having problems in your marriage, you and your spouse have a treasure stored up that is contrary to a successful marriage.

It's easy to determine the make up of your treasure by looking at the things you see in your life. You would be surprised how the devil is wreaking havoc on health, marriages, relationships, and keeping people in bondage. You can see what's inside of you by observing what's coming out of you. If you have a problem in your life, it's like a printed page from your mind. It's held up for all to read.

We live out our thinking. The importance of understanding this is not so you can figure out what's wrong with everyone else, but so you can look at yourself and see where you need to improve. I look at myself every day and think, *What did I do today that I need to improve –that I won't do tomorrow?* At the end of every day, I think, *Okay, what could I have done differently today?*

In Matthew 15:11, it says, "Not that which goeth into the mouth defileth a man; but that which cometh out of the mouth, this defileth a man." A person can be a great minister of the gospel, but can have a viper mouth in other things. It's the truth. I've seen pastors and people in ministry who are great behind the pulpit, but then they lash out like a negative viper with what they think and it just ruins their character.

"Then came his disciples, and said unto him, Knowest thou that the Pharisees were offended, after they heard this saying? But he answered and said, Every plant, which my heavenly Father hath not planted, shall be rooted up. Let them alone: they be blind leaders of the blind. And if the blind lead the blind, both shall fall into the ditch. Then answered Peter and said unto him, Declare unto us this parable. And Jesus said, Are ye also yet without understanding? Do not ye yet understand, that whatsoever entereth in at the mouth goeth into the belly, and is cast out into the draught? But those things which proceed out of the mouth come forth from the heart; and they defile the man" (Matthew 15:12-18).

Jesus went on to list the kinds of things that come from the heart. The first thing He mentioned was evil thoughts. After that, He listed murder. Now murder doesn't always entail literally killing a person. I've had people attempt to murder me by the words that have come out of their mouths. They have tried to murder my testimony or murder my character, but I'm still here. I'm not leaving.

The devil has tried to run havoc in this ministry but I'm not going to let him get one bit of foothold. I'm facing every demonic act head-on because God's sheep are more important. The best way I can help God's sheep is to show the love of God. That starts by allowing God's love to dwell in my heart so His love shows through in the words that come out of my mouth. This is the way I feel. Jesus taught His disciples important principles and through the Word, He continues to teach us today.

What is in our hearts and what comes out of our mouths affects the course of our lives. For instance, a homosexual person might say, "I was born this way. This is my nature." But that is not correct. God made man and God made woman, but God didn't make a man in a woman's body or a woman in a man's body. God does not make mistakes like that.

A person is a homosexual because he or she began to think, "Maybe I'm that way. I need to explore all the possibilities." The first little thought was a seed. The seed might have sprung from an emotional problem relating to the opposite sex or it may have been brought about by a bad relationship with a mother or father. I would say that most homosexuals have been hurt at one time or another in their lives. Those thoughts and negative emotions produce a negative and destructive homosexual lifestyle. If you are reading this book and you are a homosexual, know that we love you and we want you to overcome the thoughts that have taken root in your mind. The love of God can help you overcome. I want you to go to Heaven. You can call me at (423) 479-5434, extension 101 and we'll discuss the truth of God's love for you and what that can mean for your life..

Jesus said that murder begins with a thought. Financial problems are what tear up most homes. Where do these financial problems begin? Where do emotional dilemmas come from? All of these spring from the heart.

What I want you to see is that you can change the treasure of your heart. Once you change that treasure, you can begin to make positive withdrawals. You can bring forth new things that end the cycle of problems.

When I finally learned how to renew my mind, I could bring forth so much love. Two years ago, I just realized what the love of God truly is and it set me free. It's like a hundred pounds was lifted off of me. I was able to bring forth forgiveness, patience, and all the positive things of life.

Before I realized the truths about the love of God, my mind was negative about my mother. As a result, I brought forth a spirit of rivalry and fighting. I'd scream and lash out because of all the negative things she put me through. But once I let God put His love in my heart, I was able to remember times when she was nice to me. I'd never thought of those instances before. They suddenly just came to me.

Negative thoughts just don't fall on you. Bitterness, anger, and depression are not little clouds that float over your head and rain on you every once in a while. Sometimes, to excuse the bad things that are coming in their lives, people say, "I got up on the wrong side of the bed this morning." Others say, "Maybe, I'm just in a bad mood." But the truth is, it's not a mood. It's a way of thinking.

About three weeks ago, I got tired and felt like I'd been on the whipping post all day. But then I went home and got on my Gazelle and started praying. When I got through praying, I turned on the television and watched something funny. I took control of my thoughts and determined I would let the love of God in my heart overcome anything that might be coming against me.

When your way of thinking changes, all of your life will change. You choose what goes on in your life. You choose what you will allow into your life. Declare that the devil is not going to win in your life! The next time your children or your spouse get in a bad mood, just stand up and declare, "The devil's not winning!" It's a choice you have to make – a choice to let the love of God in your heart determine your path, a choice not to let the devil win!

# CHAPTER 5

## FIVE THINGS THAT CAN CHANGE YOU

*"And be not conformed to this world: but be ye transformed*
*by the renewing of your mind, that ye may prove what is that good,*
*and acceptable, and perfect, will of God."*

*Romans 12:2*

L ife or death - the choice is up to you. If you are experiencing cycles of defeat in your life, there are five changes you can make and these choices will change your life! In this chapter, I will share five things that can change you.

The first thing that can change you is responsibility. You have to take full responsibility for yourself. You can't blame God for your situation. If you are married, you can't blame your spouse. You can't blame anybody or anything for your situation but yourself. You can't blame the school or the church.

I'm so tired of the demonology thing—all the talk about whether there's a generational curse or not. These things do not matter! How can there still be a curse if we've been redeemed from the curse? That doesn't even make sense. The only way past devils can come at you is if you let them. You have to take responsibility for what you allow to come at you.

You have to take full responsibility for your situation. Nothing else can help you if you don't accept complete responsibility for the condition of your life. Take inventory of your life. Do you have life or do you have death? What do you have? Are all your bills paid or are they not paid? Look at your surroundings. Look at your friends. What positive things so you have in your life? Is there joy around you or are you always concentrating on something negative?

You see, until you take full responsibility, you're going to be out of control. You're going to be incapable of change. You may say, "Yeah, but they said this and they said that, and they did this to me. They act this way toward me." But the truth is, it's all you. You're the one who's responsible. The devil knows what buttons to push in you to get you. He knows which buttons to push on me, but I've determined that nobody is going to control me and force me to believe something contrary to God's truth. There's no way! I'm taking responsibility for my life – no one else!

The second thing that can change you is if you will stop and rethink what you believe and what you assume is true. You've probably heard the old saying, "I don't believe anything I hear and only half of what I see." You need to rethink your concepts for living and those things on which you base your decisions.

As you rethink the way you are living your life, you engage in the third thing that can change you. You have to reject your old destructive ways. You have to reject negative thoughts. Any negative word that has ever been said to you can't be allowed to take root. They are all lies from hell, just like the negative words that were said to me all my life. They are all lies from the devil to make you react in destructive ways. You've got to review your thoughts and meditate on the things that are positive and the things that God says are true. Then you have to speak your new thoughts out loud, so the devil can hear your new thoughts.

You can't let people bully you. You can't let people steal your joy. If they steal your joy, they steal your health. I won't let anyone steal my health. In times in my life when I have started getting a few symptoms of illness, I came to realize those symptoms didn't come from the devil. They came from me accepting the negative words people were saying.

When I rebuked those negative wordsand told the devil,"I'm not accepting them," as quickly as the symptoms came on, they left.

Such attacks are lies from hell. The devil is the father of lies. He can't speak any truth. He doesn't even know the truth. You have to reprogram your thinking, know the treasure in your heart, and understand your net worth. When you think about all the assets you have and all your liabilities, if you feel your liabilities outweigh your assets, then you need to get into the Word and reprogram your thinking.

Take control over what you're thinking. Tell the turmoil to leave. Don't put up with the devil. Don't follow the examples of those who don't have the pure treasure of the love of God in their hearts. Those people are not fit examples to look up to. Look to God and surround yourself with people who know God at least as well as you know Him.

When Pastor Bobby died, I couldn't sleep because I kept replaying the scene of him dying over and over in my mind. The doctors wanted to put me on Ambien to help me sleep, but I didn't want to depend on medicine. I knew that the key to getting the sleep I needed would be found in programming what I was thinking. I decided to take melatonin as I programmed my mind and it worked. I am a living testimony of the fact that you have to reprogram your way of thinking. You old way of thinking is not a devil. It's a habit. You have to change what's in your heart. That's where your treasure lies. You have to be strong and change your way of thinking.

A wise man told me one time, "Everywhere you go, there you are." That may sound simple, but it's really profound. You have to take yourself along everywhere you go. If you have wrong thoughts, those thoughts will create bad situations. The thoughts contained in your mind go along with you to the next situation and continue the cycle of negative outcomes.

By renewing the spirit of your mind, you can break the cycle of negative outcomes. That's the only way you can break the cycle. You have to stretch yourself to change your thinking so that your problems will not repeat and you won't have so much drama around you all the time.

The fourth thing you can do to change yourself is review. You have to review new thoughts. Mediate on a new way of thinking. When you're driving your car, instead of spacing out in your mind, think about the things of the Lord. You may say, "Well, I can't do that all the time." You've got to get control of your mind.

Sometimes, I'll be going along and I'll get the "what ifs" – "what if" this happens or "what if" they're saying this about me. That was one thing that used to really get me when I was growing up – wondering if people were talking about me. I couldn't stand it. It used to drive me crazy. The devil knows the buttons to push to get a reaction out of each of us. We can't fall prey to his schemes! We have to review and practice a new way of thinking.

The last thing you can do to change yourself and your situation is to resound. That means you speak your new thoughts so they resound out loud like this, "Oh no, I'm not taking that negative thought. I bind you devil. You get out of here in Jesus' name. You take your hands off my mind. I'm telling you right now, you can't have my mind." Do you see what I'm saying?

You have to fight for your heart. Look at this scripture, "May Christ through your faith [actually] dwell (settle down and abide, make His permanent home) in your hearts! May you be rooted deep in love and founded securely on love" (Ephesians 3:17, Amplified). Paul prayed that through your faith, Jesus would dwell in your heart and you would be grounded and rooted deeply and securely in His love.

In Ephesians 3:17, the word heart comes from a Greek word, *kardia*. That Greek word encompasses your thoughts, feelings, and mind. You're called to love God with all your heart and to serve Him first. Your heart is your mind, your thoughts, and your emotions. Your heart is where you decide what you believe in every topic.

Paul prayed that the beliefs of your heart would be centered in Christ and what He has accomplished for you. I didn't even realize what Christ had accomplished for me, until I got a true revelation of what He did that was centered in His love. That true revelation, based in His love changed me. I'm a living testimony - if I can make it in this life and still love people, then by God's love, you can too.

When I backslid and walked away from God, my heart was cold and had no love in it. I wanted to go to hell. I thought, *My Lord, there has to be better people in hell than there is in church.* That's exactly what I thought until I got a proper revelation of what Jesus did for me that was based in God's love. I don't want to go hell now. Thank God, I'm going to Heaven.

You see, the devil's plan for your heart is to steal, kill, and destroy, but the plan of Jesus is that you enjoy abundant life (John 10:10).

For the first time in my life, I got the revelation of what the love of God is and that was when He gave me this message to share with everyone. Every day you're in a fight for your heart. My prayer for you is the same as the prayer Paul prayed in Ephesians 3:17-18: "May Christ through your faith [actually] dwell (settle down and abide, make His permanent home) in your hearts! May you be rooted deep in love and founded securely on love, that you may have the power and be strong to apprehend and grasp with all the saints [God's devoted people, the experience of that love]" (AMP).

You've got to guard your heart. You cannot pay me to run around with anybody who doesn't know God as well as I do or better. I tell you, there's no money that can buy peace. I would rather be by myself. I won't even have lunch with someone who might steal my joy. Not that I'm better than anybody else, it's just that I have to watch what goes into my heart and mind. I have to watch what I see with my eyes and what I hear in my ears, because the devil gets in through your eyes and ears.

Paul goes on to pray, "[That you may really come] to know [practically, through experience for yourselves] the love of Christ, which far surpasses knowledge [without experience]; that you may be filled [through all your being] unto all the fullness of God [may have the richest measure of the Divine presence, and become

a body wholly filled and flooded with God Himself]! Now to Him Who, by (in consequence of) the [action of His] power that is at work within us, is able to [carry out His purpose and] do superabundantly, far over and above all that we [dare] ask

or think [infinitely beyond our highest prayers, desires, thoughts, hopes, or dreams] - To Him be glory in the church and in Christ Jesus throughout all generations forever and ever. Amen (so be it)" (Ephesians 3:19-21, AMP).

You see, there's a fight being waged for your heart between Jesus and the devil.

The Bible says that the thief comes but to kill, steal, and destroy. The thief – the devil – is only interested in killing you , stealing from you, and destroying you. Jesus goes on to say, "… I have come that they may have life, and that they may have it more abundantly" (John 10:10, NKJV).

Some think, "Well, this is real simple. I already know that!" Well if you know that, why are you constantly having drama in your life? Don't get lackadaisical in your faith! Don't get lackadaisical in your confession. Don't get lackadaisical in your worship. If you do, you'll dry up and you won't be any good to yourself, let alone anybody else. We've got to remember there's a fight going on and we've got to press on.

John 10:10 shows you clearly that there's two plans for your life. Whomever you choose to believe down deep in your heart will determine the course of your life. God says, "My child, pay attention to what I say…" (Proverbs 4:20, NLT). You may say, "Yeah, but you don't know the circumstances going on in my life!" Still God says, "My child, pay attention to what I say." That's what God is saying to you today. How hard is that to understand? My child, pay attention to what I say. Listen carefully to My words. Don't lose sight of what you hear. Let my words penetrate deep in your heart, for they bring life to those that find them and health to all their flesh. Guard your heart above all else, for it determines the course of your life (Proverbs 4:20-23).

How many times does God have to go over this with us? Some people keep reacting, keep getting upset, keep being insecure, and keep feeling rejected. That is a devil trying to kill your peace and joy. When he steals your joy, he also steals your strength. Proverbs 4:23 tells us, "Guard your heart above all else, for it determines the course of your life" (NLT).

When my mother left, she started another family. When my mother died, my stepfather called saying, "Forgive me. Forgive me. Forgive me. I wouldn't let her (my mother) come and see you because I was afraid I would lose her. Forgive me, forgive me, forgive me. Do you forgive me?"

I said, "Yes sir, I forgive you." I truly do forgive him. He's had a heart transplant. I've had a kidney transplant, so I feel like we have something in common. I'll call him every once in a while to check up on him. Do I always want to call him? Not always, but I don't think about it. I just do what God tells me in my heart to do, which is love everybody. I don't dwell on what happened, I just call him and ask him, "How are you feeling?"

During one of our phone conversations, I said, "Can I ask you a favor? Will you send me some pictures of my mother?"

He said, "Yes, I'll do that." So he sent the pictures. I spent about five hours looking at each picture. It took me several days to get through all of the pictures. After I had reviewed the last picture, God miraculously restored everything. It was like I knew what she was like in every picture, what mood she was in, and how she was. It was a miraculous thing. But none of that would have happened if I had allowed myself to be distracted by the devil's lies or even by what anyone else had to say.

I have to let God's Word penetrate deep in my heart. That means I have to think deeply about what He says and let His Word become the center of who I am and the core of what I believe. True abundant life is experienced when the belief of your

heart has nothing to do with what you feel, hear, or see. It has everything to do with who you are in Jesus and what God says is true about you. Circumstances are subject to change, but the truth of who you are in Jesus will remain the same.

When I learned to believe that God's words of love are true, I found out that, just as it promises in Proverbs 4:22, those words bring life and health. What does that mean? It's nothing short of a miracle. In Proverbs 4:22, that word translated "life" means, "to give promise to restore, to make whole"—it does not just mean health, but to make whole. In that same verse, the word "health" means, "a medicine or a cure, deliverance and healing." I didn't have to go through twelve steps of deliverance. I only had to listen to God.

Somebody called me about six months ago and said, "Oh, you need to listen to this woman. She gets into the root of the problem. This is what you need."

I said, "No, I don't need to listen to some woman. I need to listen to God."

Our hearts are so heavy and burdened. This is why God tells us in

Proverbs 4:23, above everything you do in life, you have to guard your heart. What you allow in your heart will become what you believe and those heart beliefs will affect your life.

Out of the beliefs of your heart will come the issues of your life. This is why you have two fighting for your heart— the Lord and the devil. Each one of them wants you to devote your thoughts to their words and believe them way down deep in your heart.

When Lucifer was made, he was called Lucifer in Heaven. When he fell, he became Satan. He was Lucifer in Heaven but when he fell, he was demoted and became Satan. His name and his position were taken from him and it's made him mad ever since. That's why it is the devil's total plan to kill, steal, and destroy you. He wants to steal your joy and peace so that your heart will be filled with shame, insecurity, and fear. He wants you to experience loss just like he did. Misery loves company.

Don't let the devil steal your peace. Don't let the devil steal your joy. Jesus wants to bring your heart to Him. Let Him fill your mind and thoughts with His words of love—the love of God—the true love of God. Break free from the devil's lies.

Paul warned us in the Scriptures of the devil's plan to deceive your heart using the exact same tactics he used on Eve. When he approached Eve, he tricked her by getting her to doubt what God said. You've been told by Jesus that you're good and that He approves of you completely. Paul feared that in the very same way Eve was deceived, the devil would try to deceive you into believing that you're not good enough and that you're not who God says you are.

I used to be bashful — if you can believe that, but I overcame it. I wanted to start my own business teaching aerobics. Now at the time, nobody knew me from Adam's house cat except the people at the courthouse and at the bank. But I put an ad in the paper advertising my aerobic classes at the community center. I started teaching two nights a week, Tuesdays and Thursdays. It went over so well, I started teaching three nights a week. I added an earlier class at 6:00, before my regular 7:00 classes. It went over so well, I added 5:00 classes.

I started looking at some of the girls in the class and saw how well they could keep up with the routine. Eventually, I started offering six classes a day, three days a week, and I had some of those girls come in and lead the additional classes. I was offering classes for mentally handicapped kids and retired women, in addition to all the other classes. We offered classes at 11:00, 12:00, 4:00, 5:00, 6:00, 7:00, and 8:00 and I had nine girls working for me.

I tell you this story to say, you can do whatever you have in your mind to do if you say, "I'm going to do this." I used to be bashful, but I'm not bashful anymore. The thing is, I set it in my mind and in my heart what I wanted to do, believing that because God loves me, I could do it. You have to set things in your mind and in your heart— positive things. There's nothing you can't do. There's nothing you can't accomplish.

In order to guard your heart from the devil's lies, you've got to recognize when you're being tempted to believe a lie. Every lie that the devil throws at you produces negative emotions. Once, I had a couple of students who were far out in left field. I got their numbers and I tried to call them a few times. They wouldn't even answer the phone. I left messages but they never returned my calls. This discouraged me.

One day, I sat in my office and said, "Lord, I know that the devil is a liar. I'm not going to take the fact that they won't return my calls personally, but at this moment, honestly, I feel like quitting. You need to strengthen me by Your grace. I'm asking You to strengthen me by Your grace." Thank goodness Jesus is so faithful to run to our assistance when we humbly turn to Him—every time! He strengthened me once again with the promises of His Word. I rejected the devil's lies and went to the truth of the Word of God.

You can encourage yourself in God's Word. At that time, I didn't need a bunch of people who work with me to encourage me. I found out that I was able to encourage myself in the Lord and began to thank Him for His faithfulness in all He had promised me. I resisted the devil by saying, "Devil, you're a liar and you're a deceiver. My heart belongs to Jesus and I choose to believe what He says about me. Thank You, Lord, that You're causing my thoughts to be agreeable to Your will in everything I put my hand to do. I'm going to prosper and be a success. You create life in me and you give me the desire and the power to carry out Your will for my life. You've anointed me to share, preach, and teach the gospel, and to encourage the ones the devil is trying to deceive."

Guard your heart from the enemy's lies and fill it with God's truth. Without fail, every time I turn my heart to Jesus and allow Him to fill my thoughts with His truth,

I'm set free from the devil's lies. They cannot affect my heart. The same can be true for you.

You need not fear the schemes of the devil. A curse can never come on you—ever! It's not allowed to come on you. You're covered in the blood of Jesus. Curses, hexes, or witchcraft words have no authority over you.

Jesus wants you to live free from fear. He wants you to live free from low self-esteem. He wants you to live free from insecurity.

You may ask, "Well, what about your cousin who was a homosexual? Did you love him?" Yes, I showed him the love of God. God loved him. My cousin just had a flesh problem. But before he died, he accepted Jesus into his heart. You may think that's impossible that God would love my cousin and come into his heart, because he was a homosexual. Is that where you draw the line—the love of God can't extend to a homosexual? Wrong! The love of God extends to everyone who will accept it into their hearts. I know my cousin went to Heaven.

Everybody has a past filled with things that they've done. Every scar you have is proof that you've come through something. Scars come with healing, so every scar you have should serve as a reminder of the healing you've received as you came out on the other side. You see, Jesus has rescued you from the devil's kingdom that is filled with darkness and lies, and He's brought you into His Kingdom.

You see, when your heart is filled with negative emotion, you have to turn to Jesus and ask Him to help you believe the truth. That's the only way you're going to be abundantly free. The opposite of freedom is condemnation and that's what you get when you have a negative opinion of yourself. That devil of negativity will always try to come back! Don't dare accept him back, because if you do, just like Scripture warns, it will come back seven times worse than before it left (Luke 11:24-26).

Don't accept anything the devil says about you. Reject his lies and fill your heart with the truth and love of God.

Many years ago, the devil tried to put me in fear of dying. When I was in

Sheffield, Alabama, he came out from behind a curtain, pointed his hand at me and said, "I'm going to kill you." I said, "No, you're not. In Jesus name, you go from me." This happened in 1977.

After that, I would go in the bathroom and turn the shower on, and it would feel like an evil spirit was walking behind me. Then I'd hear his voice saying, "I'm killing you." The only reason I made it through is because I realized that the Holy Spirit is with me always. I should have automatically rejected these attacks. After all, the devil is the father of lies. Why would I believe him on anything? You cannot believe him at all. You have to guard your heart.

When my husband Terry went in the hospital, I realized that the Holy Spirit was with him. I knew that the devil couldn't get to him. I really didn't feel grieved in my spirit. I'm so thankful for what Jesus does. He always shows up on the scene! Though Terry was pronounced dead two times, the Lord brought him back. I know beyond a shadow of a doubt that I do not need to fear anything – not even death. God's love and truth in my heart revealed this to me.

At one time or another in our lives, we've all let the devil take over and we've become offended, felt rejected, or been discouraged because somebody said or did this or that. But it doesn't matter what somebody did. All that matters is what Jesus did. He laid down His life for you—totally laid down His life!

We have to guard our hearts. We can be empowered by grace to say first thing when we get out of bed in the morning, "Devil, I serve you notice." God is there first thing in the morning and He is empowering you from the first moment you awake to guard your heart. Don't let the devil talk you into hurting yourself. The devil knows how to push your buttons. Keep the joy because as long as you keep the joy, you'll have strength. I don't care what anybody tries to push on you, if it's not in the Word of God, don't buy it.

# CHAPTER 6

## UNCONDITIONAL LOVE

*"These things I command you, that ye love one another."*

*John 15:17*

There is no natural love that compares to the love of God, not even the love shared between husband and wife and family. You may think you love your family that much, but it's an unconditional love that God gives that surpasses anything man is capable of giving. If we

mess up, He never leaves us.

So many people make all their problems, finances, and hurts bigger than the Word of God. The devil seeks to make these things bigger even than the Word of God to you, but they are not. Now, you can't just casually look through the Word and expect that it will dwarf all of your problems. You have to read it and meditate on it. You have to get it inside of you.

In John 15:17, God tells us to love one another. Now, that's a command! The scripture continues, "If the world hate you, ye know that it hated me before it hated you. If ye were of the world, the world would love his own: but because ye are not of the world, but I have chosen you out of the world, therefore the world hateth you" (John 15:18-19). God has chosen you. It doesn't matter what you've done, He has still chosen you. That's unconditional love.

However, the world hates you. If you have had problems and failures in your life, it's because the world hates you and the devil hates you. The devil wants to destroy your life. By he knows that if the Lord can get you to dedicate yourself to Him and realize that He loves you unconditionally, then, you'll be a threat to him.

At one time when I was plagued by sickness, I was laying in the hospital bed and my legs were swollen. The medical professionals were wrapping my legs with bandages, like they would do to the legs of a horse. When I would walk, I walked stiffly. One day, I said to the devil, "You know what? I coming out of this and my heel is going to bruise your brow, and I will never stop. Do you understand me? I'm never going to stop."

The more I said that, the more the devil attacked me. The devil said, "No, I am going to kill you. I got you this time. I'm going to kill you." One night, I was sitting on the side of the bed at midnight when Terry came in and said, "Okay, we're going to the hospital because you're not going to die." I went to the hospital and had six pounds of fluid removed from my lungs.

The Bible tells the story of a father who had a son who was possessed by a mute spirit. The father brought the boy to Jesus and said, "If thou canst do any thing, have compassion on us, and help us" (Mark 9:22). This was Jesus' reply to that father: "If thou canst believe, all things are possible to him that believeth" (Mark 9:23). Did you see that? This same message is for you. If you can believe, all things are possible. It doesn't matter what it is that you need, all things are possible.

Even if you rejected God and fled from God or maybe you fell for an idol, whether it be pot, sex, lying, stealing, etc., God did not reject you. Rather, God pursues you. God pursues you because He loves you and this love is not based on what you did or did not do. His love is based on His character. His character is unconditional love.

Consider the words of 1 John 4:10: "In this is love, not that we loved God, but that He loved us and sent His Son to be the propitiation for our sins" (NKJV). He loved us first. The Bible says in Ephesians 2:4-5, "But God, who is rich in mercy, because of His great love with which He loved us, even when we were dead in trespasses, made us alive together with Christ (by grace you have been saved)" (NKJV). Even when we were still sinners, God loved us first.

The love of God is not an idea or mystical thought that brings out the best in you. It's an action that is revealed and defined because of the coming of the Lord Jesus Christ into the world to take our place in death. Because of His great love for us, He suffered and died on the cross, was buried, rose from the dead, and is now seated at the right hand of the throne of God.

As He is sitting at the right hand of the throne of God, He hears me when I'm kneeling on my knees, or laying on my bed, or sitting in a chair, or sitting in my car. When I say, "Jesus, I'm telling You right now, I need Your help. I need for You to be my lawyer, my advocate." He hears my cry and goes to the Father on my behalf.

Jesus Christ is the dictionary of Heaven. He defines God's love and gives us revelation of the nature of that love. I don't fully understand how God can love us so much, but I know that He does and I know that His love in our hearts can enable us to love others, just like it enabled me to love my mother all those years after she abandoned me. I received a revelation of the love of God.

At one time or another, we've all been separated from the love of God - like sheep lost in the wilderness. I watched a film recently about animals. In the film, a herd of buffalo are being stalked by lions. The lions were hunched down looking at the buffalo. I don't think the buffalo could see them because they were walking slowly, casually like there was nothing about which to panic. Suddenly, the lions attacked a baby buffalo from the herd, took it and ran into a river.

The lions were trying to kill the baby buffalo, but were having a hard time tearing through the tough buffalo skin. As they were trying to kill the buffalo, all of a sudden, a crocodile came up and attacked the lions. In the struggle, the lions ran back up on land, accompanied by the baby buffalo. The next thing you know, about thirty buffalo came on the scene and rescued the baby buffalo, taking him back into the herd.

As I watched that film, I couldn't help but think that's what Jesus does when somebody goes astray. He's a jealous God. The Bible says that the shepherd declares when he finds his lost sheep, "Rejoice with me; for I have found my sheep which was lost" (Luke 15:6). If you mess up, so what? He doesn't ever stop loving you; He doesn't ever stop searching for you to bring you back to Himself. .All of His sheep mean something to Him. You're His sheep. You're valuable to Him.

When we're lost from God, our Shepherd, we're in a world of isolation and abandonment. We're desperate to find a place of love and security. That's why so many people look for love in wrong places. They're trying to fulfill that need for love and security.

The Shepherd searches for His sheep, but He does so in a non-judgmental way. I know this to be true. He was looking for me, but I didn't want Him to find me. I was trying to hide in my bedroom, not wanting Him to see me and what I was doing. Then I thought, *This is stupid. He knows where I am.*

The truth is, He saves us and doesn't condemn us. Unconditional love does not mean that He will excuse, cover, or lie for us. Unconditional love does not make excuses for our wrong behavior. But it does seek to bring us back without condemning us for what we've done.

God doesn't say that something is wrong with our genes or that we're sick and therefore not responsible for our actions. It's stupid to think that you don't have to be held responsible for your actions. The sheep is not allowed to wander aimlessly in a pasture of its choice. In the same way, the Good Shepherd does not leave you to wander aimlessly in your own ignorance.

God's unconditional love does not mean that He has thrown away truth. We may live in a world where everybody is considered right by default, but that doesn't make it so. The fact that the Good Shepherd has to search for His lost sheep means that they have gone astray. The fact that you're under conviction is evidence that there's something wrong.

But God is not going to bash you over the head with your mistakes. He's not out to condemn you. He seeks to bring you back to a place of safety, a home for the sheep. There's a home where His sheep are meant to be and a way of life that brings them peace that passes all understanding.

When we receive the love of God, it's our responsibility to pass on that love to others. You have to show love. Tell somebody you love them every day, especially people who have experienced rejection, people who came from a bad past. Every day, you have to tell someone you love them. It doesn't matter what they do, you have to tell them you love them. If somebody does wrong over and over, you must never get tired of telling that person that you love them. That's unconditional love.

I'm not a religious person. I don't believe in religion. I'm not really spiritual. I just love God. I have experienced the real love of God. Religion says you can be good enough, but you can't work your way to earning God's approval. God loves everybody the same.

Why did the good Shepherd come to live among us? It was because man would have been forever separated from God unless there was a divine intervention. He entered into our lostness and died for our sins to show the infinite extent of our wrongness. Why did somebody have to die on a cross for humanity to be saved? Because that's how lost we were – we deserved death. Jesus said that He came for those who were sick. He pointed out that if no one were sick, there'd be no reason for a divine doctor to make house calls. Thank God Jesus makes house calls!

The unconditional love of God is what prompted Him to send His

Son to bring back the sheep. He does not come to kill the sick sheep. If you've praying for somebody for years, only to have them die, know that the Lord did not kill them. Almost all the time, the reason why people die is because they're tired and worn out. Their death doesn't have anything to do with your faith or their faith. Never forget that God's love is unconditional. The Lord does not come to kill the sick and rebellious sheep, but to save and heal them through a relationship with Himself. Only in His presence are we made whole.

Jesus, the love of God in flesh, confronts us with the unconditional love of the Father. He doesn't sweep our sin under the rug, but He brings it out in the open and confronts us with it. He confronts us with the fact that we're separated from the one who is our life. You see, we are dead in our sin. But through our salvation found in the resurrection of Jesus Christ, we are given new life. That's what getting saved is all about.

When we are born into this world, we are born into sin. I was a loser before I got saved, but I'm not a loser now. I can't do anything to be a loser. Jesus Christ has saved me and there is no way He'll turn against me. When I opened the door and asked Jesus to come into my heart, from that point on there was nothing I could do to be a loser in His eyes.

Jesus is the Word. He is the unconditional love of God in the flesh and when He died, He was identified with our sin. He was punished for our rebellion and our shame. Because of what He did - when we identify ourselves with Him in His death, burial and resurrection; when we get saved – He says that we can do more than He did when He was on this earth.

He arose from the dead because He achieved His end. The law had been satisfied and man's debt for sin was paid on the cross. Because of that selfless act, thank God, we're completely pardoned. We're now able to embrace the love of God. We once were dead in our sins and lost, but the good news is that you and I are loved and we're pardoned.

We're welcome into the family of God. God, by definition, is complete by Himself. He doesn't need to have angels. He doesn't need to have anything. He's complete by Himself, but He chose to create you and desired from the start that you would be part of His family.

Repentance is a word that simply means a change of mind. It's real simple—just changing your mind. Faith means that you abandon attempts to find meaning within yourself and instead rest completely in God and His love. When you respond to God's love, it requires a change of mind. When you hear the good news of God's unconditional love, you have to change your mind. When I changed my mind and realized that God loves me, I felt the shock waves of this truth reach to the innermost parts of me. Those shock waves blasted every demon of rejection, every demon of judgment, every demon of exaggeration, and every demon of negativity right out of me.

I realized for the first time that God is not a monster as I thought Him to be, but He is the best friend I could ever have and He loves me no matter what happens. I don't have to prove anything to anybody. I don't have to work myself half to death. I don't have to do anything for Him to love me.

God spoke to me and told me to read seven times the book, *How to Live and Not Die*. He was getting me ready for what was to come, so I would be prepared. I did exactly what He told me to do, but then I realized that reading this book had a ritual. I had begun to think that I would not get my healing unless I read that book every day.

God said to me, "Zona, I didn't give you your miracle because you read *How to Live and Not Die*. I prepared you. I was warning you that the enemy was going to attack. You only had to listen to what I said. It's all about you loving Me. Everything stems from that. I bore your sickness; I bore your pain. The chastisement of your peace is upon me, and by the stripes I bore on my back, you are healed. You have to have a revelation of that. It doesn't take but a pepper speck of faith in that truth to heal you."

He reminded me of when Dave Roberson prophesied to me in 1992. I was standing up and we were worshipping the Lord. Dave said, "There's going to be an onslaught attack of the devil and it's is going to try to kill you, but if you will not look to the left or to the right, but only look straight ahead to Me, you'll live—you'll make it."

During that time of onslaught, I would call Dave. I did this for over three years and I would ask him, "Now, what did He say?" Dave would tell me, "I said that the Lord said, if you will not look to the left or to the right, but you'll look straight ahead, you'll come through." I had to call Dave over and over to be reminded of what God promised me.

But when I realized the truth of God's unconditional love and changed my mind about me to admit that the way I was living my life was wrong, my whole mindset changed. At the time, I was preaching the gospel and yet I had to admit that I was wrong. When you change your mind about the very meaning of life and surrender yourself to God's unconditional love, it becomes clear that the only reason you're on earth is to be loved by God. Apart from God, none of us are a big deal. It's an honor and a privilege that He God chose us and that He loves us. He wants to demonstrate His love in our lives.

The Lord called me and I am going to do what He has called me to do. One day, my dad was sitting in the chair right across from my desk and he said, "I just can't believe what God has done in your life. I know everybody has a testimony, but what you have been through, it was like a thousand times magnified because when a person really feels like nobody loves them, you can't control them." We promised each other that day that we would keep that fire to tell others about the Word and about God's unconditional love built up on the inside of ourselves. You see, you have to build yourself up in the Most Holy faith.

You can't treat people just any way you want to treat them. You have to be good to people. You have to show them God's unconditional love. You can't talk to them just any way you want to talk to them. You can't cuss people. You can't use words that tear people down. We have to do this because of the unconditional love God has shown us.

I want to please the Lord, just because I love Him so much. I love Him a thousand times more because of what He's done for me and what He's brought me out of. Many times, He has saved me from death itself. I've been told I only had 24 hours to live, told I had only six months or a year to live. This happened twelve times! But God's unconditional love saved me from it all, which is why I'm not giving up.

You have to be strong in the Lord, in the power of His might, praying in the Holy Ghost. Be fully persuaded that God will do what He says He will do in His Word—fully persuaded, not partially. I'm fully persuaded. I trust Him. I believe Him. I love Him. That wasn't always the case. In the past, I just said I loved Him because you're supposed to say you love God when you're a Christian. But when you have a revelation of the true unconditional love of God, it's so different. Things change on the inside and the love you feel for God and others grows.

*It's Been Love All Along*

# CHAPTER 7

## GOD'S LOVE SURPASSESS EVERYTHING

*"(Love)…hopes all things, endures all things.*
*Love never fails."*

*1 Corinthians 13:7-8, NKJV*

There are three words that contain the answer to every question and articulated fear that you have on the inside of you. These words are food for your body. Having an understanding of these three words means that you'll never be shackled by despair ever again. You won't have to put up with tiredness in your body, no matter what kind of day you've had. These three words are your answer.

You'll never have to wallow in the belief that you are worthless or that you've made mistakes that are forever inexcusable. You no longer have to carry the burden of what you've done in the past or feel like you have lived a meaningless existence in this world.

These three little words are life-bringing words and they will get you through everything. Homes will be reconciled. The Lord will give you ideas to make money. You'll have peace in your mind. You won't be just doing your own thing. These three little words are the most important things in your life. You can have teachings on worship, prosperity, the mercy of God, the grace of God, how to be an overcomer, and walking by faith, but these words are over all. These three words are *God is love!*

To know the love of God and to know the love that God has for you, is the answer to every spiritual thing that you might long for. It is the source of healing for all mental and physical dysfunction –

healing for the body, healing for the mind, healing for relationships. It doesn't matter what happened to you when you were young or if people stabbed you in the back, lied to you and stole from you. It doesn't matter! It doesn't matter how many mistakes you've made The truth contained in these three words – "God is love" - will get you through every day for the rest of your life.

It doesn't matter how much of the knowledge of God you have. It doesn't matter if you can quote three-fourths of the Bible. It doesn't matter how many people have been healed when you've laid your hands on them. It doesn't matter how much you've prophesied. If you don't have an understanding of the truth of these three little words - "God is love" – none of that matters.

Comprehending these three words means that you can know without a shadow of a doubt that God loves you. The words, "God is love," are the strong and solid foundation you need on which to base your life.

I shared these words with a woman and she turned to me and just snarled. She

said, "Don't be stupid! How could God in His right mind love me? I'm worthless! Look what I've done. Look at what I've thought. Look at the things I've said. I'm garbage, Zona. I've had three abortions. You just don't understand. I'm garbage, Zona. I have MS. I'm in a bed. I'm crippled. I'm garbage, Zona. Do you not understand? I've went with married men. I've done pot. I've done drugs. Do you hear me? I haven't done one thing in my life to give me reason to believe that God could ever love me. The only person I know who loves me is you. You've never turned against me— never, never, never, since we graduated from high school."

I could relate to where this woman was coming from. Many of us have said words like this at one time or another. If we haven't said them, then we've thought them.

When I talk about God's love, most people tell me they can't even grasp what I'm am saying. They look at their behavior, their thoughts, things they have gone through or are going through, they look at their own human nature and they think there is no way God can love them.

Many people defend themselves by saying they've done the best they could do under the circumstances. Yet even in saying this, they do not believe it is possible for them to be in a good place with God. I see good in everybody, but that's not what makes it possible for us to experience the love of God. He loves us not because of what we've done, but be cause He IS love

Recently, I was talking to a minister on the phone and when our conversation was over, this minister thought he had hung up the phone, but he had not. He did not know I was still on the line and that I could hear him cussing in the background. I just hung up the phone to disconnect the call. When I did that, all of a sudden his phone starting beeping and the minister realized he had forgotten to hang up. When he remembered that I was the last one he had talked to and that I probably had overheard him cussing, he came to me crying and repenting. I simply said, "I love you. That was a flesh problem. That's not who you are. Let's just start over."

I've seen so many believers who have said the sinner's prayer and believe they're going to go to Heaven, but they still wallow in feelings of worthlessness. People say, "Well, you don't understand. The reason they feel worthless is because they don't understand the grace of God." I always reply that it's not that they don't understand the grace of God – it's that they don't understand the *love* of God. We're not talking about grace right now. We're talking about love, which is grace.

The love of God wipes everything away. Past things don't matter. God's love gives you a chance to start over. It doesn't matter if you lost it yesterday or if you had bad thoughts yesterday. The love of God gives you a chance to start fresh each day.

It's very important that you worship God both at home and at church. Do you know why worship is so important? When you worship God, you're able to get free of anything else and focus on God. Worship frees you from other things that might distract you from the truth of God. Worship helps you remember the truth that God is love.

It doesn't matter what people do to you, it cannot change the truth that God is love. I've had people do everything to me, but I don't turn against people. People get upset over the least little thing. They get frustrated. But there's no reason to get upset and frustrated. God takes you just like you are. He loves you right where you are.

God meets you where you're at. You don't have to conjure up and dress up. He meets you right where you are at. It doesn't matter what people say or how they judge you. God loves you. He knows everything about you and He loves you still. You cannot do anything in secret. He knows every single thing you've done. You can lie to people, but you cannot lie to God. He knows if your heart is real and sincere.

There have been many who, in the eyes of people, have been considered "hopeless cases." But to God, there are no hopeless cases. If anyone finds himself without hope, it is his choice to live as hopeless. It is not God's choice because God never stops loving—ever. He's the one I've had to count on when it seemed all hope was lost.

I once felt so alone, like a freak. I felt so alone, but I knew the Holy Spirit dwelled inside me. I knew that in my darkest moments—and I've had a lot of dark moments - He was the only one who could get me through. The same is true for you. God is the only one who can get you through when it seems there is no way. He's the only one. Your pastor, parents or spouse can do things physically to take care of you, but down deep in your spirit - in your heart - Jesus is the only one you can count on.

I want to get this branded in your heart. I want you to have a full understanding of the words, "God is love." The following verses are probably very familiar to you. You've probably been reading them since you were saved, but I want you to take a fresh look at this passage today. "Though I speak with the tongues of men and of angels, but have not love, I have become sounding brass or a clanging cymbal" (1 Corinthians 13:1, NKJV). This verse is talking about the God-kind of love—not natural love. You see, when you're married, you should love your spouse. But if you only love him or her with natural love, you'll be fussing all the time as everything the other does will get on your nerves. You must learn to love your spouse, your children, and even people who did you wrong with the God-kind of love. That kind of love can endure the test of time.

I'm not trying to boast or brag on myself, but I believe that the Lord has given me a gift to love people with a God-kind of love. I really believe that with all my heart. But this ability is something that God has to give you. It's not something you can work up on your own.

I look at how God has given me the ability to forgive my mother as proof of what He can do. Sometimes, I'll just be getting ready to come to the church or I'll be working out or even watching a movie, doing something that I'm not even thinking about, and all of sudden, the scent of the wood closet my mother used to lock me in will come to mind and I can smell it. The natural tendency would be to get angry or depressed – to let those old feelings creep in. Yet God has enabled me to love her with His kind of love, instead. The work that He has done in my heart enabling me to love my mother with His kind of love, has also helped me to love others.

Now, I'm not perfect. You might be the smartest person in the world and have all knowledge, all kinds of degrees, have been around people and helped them all your life, but you're nothing without God's love. The passage goes on to say, "And though

I have the gift of prophecy, and understand all mysteries and all knowledge, and though I have all faith, so that I could remove mountains, but have not love, I am nothing. And though I bestow all my goods to feed the poor, and though I give my body to be burned, but have not love, it profits me nothing" (I Corinthians 13:2-3, NKJV). It doesn't matter how nice you are, how generous, how smart, if you don't have the love of God in your heart, it means nothing.

The Bible goes on to give a description of love. It says that love "suffereth long" (1 Corinthians 13:4). Do you understand what that means? Love doesn't give up easily. It's in it for the long term. Verses four and five also tell us that love is kind, it does not envy, it does not parade itself around, it is not stuck up, does not behave rudely, and does not seek its own. Love expects and believes the best about others. It doesn't think evil things about everybody. Verse six tells us that love rejoices in the truth. If you've messed up, don't cover it up. Just say, "I've messed up." Verse seven tells us that love bears all things, believes all things, hopes all things, endures all things. Love still loves, even when others have messed up. It believes that there is good in everybody. If someone messes up, see good in them still.

Verse eight says that love never fails. Do you understand that love is the answer to everything? Pray for God's love to abide in your heart. Don't give to get. Don't do things for others just so they'll do things for you. Do for others, give to others, and love others because you have God on the inside of you. You know that He is your Savior.

You see, sometimes we say, "Oh yeah, I've been saved," but folks can't tell it by the way we live. You can't do whatever you want to do when you get saved—really saved. You have to live a holy life with no hidden agendas and no hidden things of the heart.

The love of God is a free gift! I can't even fully comprehend the love of God. He loves us regardless. When I was on drugs, one day I fell on my knees in a concrete parking lot. I pointed up to Heaven and said, "God, I will never serve You another day in my life. I would rather go to hell than serve You. You took my mother away. You've taken my daddy away. I'm never serving You again."

When I said those words, I felt myself become hard in my heart because of all the hurt. It was over. Forget it. I wouldn't go down the religious road again. I'd seen too much. I'd seen preachers who were committing adultery in the pulpit, using my dad for money, and just not living Christian the life. I saw them partying in a club, then they would preach on Sunday. I said, "Not me." I wanted no part of that.

My dad was always a businessman and then he became a businessman and minister, helping so many people. One day I went home, looked at him as he was packing his suitcase and said, "Well, where you going today? You going to New York? You going to Texas? You going to Kentucky? Where are you going? Boy, don't it make you feel good that you can help all these other people, but I know you can't do a thing for me."

I can't believe I talked to my dad that way! I had to have been nuts. He turned around and said, "Well, you're a disgrace, I can't believe you're doing this. You haven't been raised to do this. What's wrong with you? You're nothing but trash. I can't even believe this." I said, "I thought that's how you'd react."

My dad went on to Brother Kenneth Hagin's house. The Hagins were Dad's mentors and they were just wonderful people. While he was there, Sister Goodwin gave a prophecy to my dad. The Lord told her to tell him, "The thing that you want the most in the world (for me to come back to the Lord) will never happen because she's gone too far into darkness. When she comes in at 3:00 or 4:00 in the morning, what I want you to do every time you see her is simply tell her you love her, then shut up. Right now, she doesn't believe anybody loves her—not anybody."

Dad returned from the Hagin's a changed man. When the Lord first told him this word, Dad said, "What, do You mean I don't love her? I love Zona." That's when the Lord said, "She doesn't believe anybody loves her."

Have you been in that situation? Have you felt so alone that you just didn't believe that anybody loved you. That's a horrible situation to be in. I have been there, I know how you feel.

Dad came back a changed man. I was hard-core unloveable. It might have been 4:00 in the morning but when Dad heard me come in, he would say, "Little Zona, come here." I would go to his door and I'd just say, "What?"

He would say, "Come here. Stand by my bed." To which I would reply, "What do you want? What?"

He would then say, "I want to tell you that I love you and I want to tell you that Jesus loves you." My only response was, "Yeah, right? Is that it?" He would then say, "That's it," and I'd turn around and walk out.

I'd get up the next day and Dad would be getting ready. As I was getting ready to leave for work and he'd say, "Zona, I want to tell you something."

I would ask, "What do you want?" He would reply, "I want to tell you I love you and Jesus loves you." I would then say, "Whatever," and I'd walk out. It was the same thing every day.

After about six months, we reached the point where he would go, "Hey Zona, come here." I'd say, "What do you want? Are you going tell me you love me again and Jesus loves me? Yeah, right. I just said it. Do you have to say it too?"

By that time, he'd be gritting his teeth but he would still say, "I love you Zona, and Jesus loves you."

Then one day, I was sitting in the living room and I started to believe what my dad had been telling me. I was getting ready to go to the club and I said, "Hey Dad, come in here a minute." He said, "Okay honey," and he came in there.

I said, "Sit down. I just want you to know that I know the people I run with don't love me. They don't even love themselves, so how can they love me? I really don't want to go tonight, but Daddy, I know you love me." My dad started crying, then I said, "But I'm just going to go."

He said, "You don't have to go. You can stay here with me. Oh little Zona, stay here with me. What is God going to have to do to bring you back to Him?"

I replied, "He'll have to knock me in my head because I'm not going to go back to Him. I don't want to serve God. Too much is messed up. I don't want to go down that road. All those people are so two-faced; I just don't want to go down that road."

Dad told me, "It doesn't have anything to do with the people, but it has everything to do with your relationship with Him." To this I said, "Well, I'm just not going to serve Him. He'll just have to knock me in the head, I guess."

Right after that, I heard a horn sound outside so I went out. As my friends and I were pulling out of the driveway, Dad stood on the porch, pointed to the car and said, "Devil, you can't have my daughter. Lord, you heard what Zona said, that You'd have to knock her in the head. I give You permission to do whatever You want to do. Shake her foundation. Shake it."

I didn't drink that night. I didn't do any drugs that night. I was totally sober. I knew where I was. I came in about 3:00 in the morning. I didn't want anybody to know that I was home, so I came in very quietly. I was coughing so I took a pillow and was coughing in the pillow so Dad wouldn't hear me. I decided not to go to my room, but instead decided I would sleep in the guest bedroom. What I did not know is that Dad had laid his hands on the guest bed and prayed.

I went to the guest room and lay down on one of the twin beds. I didn't know it was the bed Dad had put his hands on. After I lay down on the bed and went to sleep, about 5:00 in the morning, I turned over and my eyes were even with a belt buckle.

The Lord says that sometimes angels are dressed in bright clothing. Let me tell you, sometimes they wear belt buckles! My eyes were even with this guy's belt buckle as I was laying on the bed. I looked up and I tried to scream, but I couldn't get any noise out. He was sitting Indian-style on the floor. He put his right leg over his left, turned around, and got up. It seemed like he was as big as three men. I was trying to scream, but I couldn't scream. I thought the devil was coming after me. I didn't know it was an angel.

He stood up and just looked at me. Then he turned and walked around the bed through the wall. I heard him walking down the linoleum floor. I got up out of the bed and looked out the door, but there was nothing there. I went down the hall, turned past the kitchen at the doorway, and then looked around. There he was, waiting on me, and then he just walked through the wall. I was hysterical but I couldn't get out any noise. I ran back to my dad's room, knocked on the door and softly said, "Dad. Dad."

He called my name and opened the door. He said I was as white as a ghost and my eyes were wide and I couldn't get a complete sentence out. I said, "Man. No, no, not man. I, I, I…don't know…what it was."

Dad just looked at me and started smiling. He said, "Zona, that was your angel."

I said, "I don't want him. He's too big."

He said, "He goes with you everywhere."

I said, "No, I don't want him. I want a little one with wings." At that time, I still didn't give my heart back to the Lord. I was hard, but because of the love of God shown through my dad and because Jesus loved me enough to send an angel into my room, I never took drugs again. It scared everything out of me.

A year and a half later, I gave my heart to the Lord because I couldn't get away from the love of God. I kept thinking, *God loves me that much. He loves me that much!*

I'm telling you, the love of God surpasses everything. The freedom you have now is because of the love of God. You have to see past the wrongs of people. You have to see past people's past. You have to see past people's hurts. You have to see past them.

The love of God changed my dad and it can do the same for you. The love of God can change you and change members of your family. So many people say, "My father did this or my mother did this." You might say, "I don't love my parents; I don't even know them." That's where I was. I fully understand where you're coming from, which is why I can tell you that the love of God works miracles. I didn't know my mother. I wouldn't have known her if she'd walked in the room with me. But once I experienced the full love of God, I took little steps to love her. I started sending flowers every Mother's Day. Every Christmas, I would go to the jewelry store and I would send her a piece of jewelry. I don't know if she liked anything I sent or not.

For fifteen years, from the time I was thirteen years old, I never got a response and never got a gift from my mother. I never got a card or a letter. But by faith, I was determined to love and honor my mother.

God's love in my heart game me the strength and faith I needed to love my mother. I'm sure my dad had to walk by faith to love me. That's for sure! The world has nothing like this to offer. God along can offer the unconditional love necessary to strengthen your faith to love others. I thank God for everything He's done for me. I thank Jesus for His love!

You've got to be strong and stay strong and realize that you are abundantly free because of the love of God. With the trying times that are coming, you've got to get in the Word, stay in the Word, and be confident in who you are in Christ Jesus. I know that I'm abundantly free and you've got to know that you're abundantly free because of the sacrifice of the Messiah, made because of His great love for you. You've got to get a revelation of His blood poured out on the altar of the cross.

We're a free people. We're free of penalties and punishment - abundantly free. God provided for everything we could possibly need. When I read the scriptures concerning God's love and reflect on this revelation of God's love that has filled my heart to such a degree that tears fill my eyes, my heart is filled with so much love for my Savior. I had read about God's love all my life and had been taught it all my life,

but it took me so many years to truly get this revelation of God's love. You'd think that as long as I've been around the ministry, having heard Brother Hagin, Brother Sumrall, Brother Osteen, Brother Dave and so many other great men of God preach, you would think that I would have had this revelation of God's love, but it's something you have to experience for yourself.

When you put your trust in God and His love, you don't have to pay for your sins anymore. Thank God, by His love shown in the shed blood of Jesus, the price has been paid. You can be free from shame.

Those four years that I was backslid, seemed more like fifteen years. I can't even believe it when I think about some of the things I did. I studied the drugs, went to the doctor and stole his prescription pad. I learned to write like he does so I could write my own prescriptions. Then I would go into a pharmacy and have those prescriptions filled. That took a lot of nerve. I could have gone to jail! When I think about the things I have done, shame and condemnation could easily come to my heart. Condemnation is the opposite of freedom.

When I was trying to get off drugs, I knelt down and prayed, "I don't even know if You're there, God, but I'm telling You right now, You're going to have to help me! I can't do this. I can't let my family know that I'm hooked on this. I can't let my family know that I need to go to rehab. This has got to be a secret between me and You. You have got to help me."

God knew that my heart was real and open before Him. The problem is that in Bible schools, some students like to look clean on the outside, but inside, they like porn and like to gossip. Gossip is as bad as porn. That demon is still running loose because the students are not ready to minister. They are trying to minister to the soup kitchen people in the field before they have been open and honest with God about their own lives. You have to be ready to minister to people. You just can't let everybody run out and minister to people. Ministers need to be prepared. Until students dedicate themselves to change, they will not be prepared to minister. Bible School itself will not change them.

When they fall in love with God and get the God-kind of love deep on the inside of them, it will change them. Look at some of the pastors standing behind the pulpit todeay. Some are secret drinkers, having an affair with their secretary, or some are even homosexuals. The devil is running rampant trying to destroy Christian homes. People live in farce marriages. All of this is a result of believing the devil's lies. He wants to convince you that you are not who God says you are because of your past failures. It's a lie! He wants to convince you that you really don't deserve God's blessing because you haven't been good enough.

But the devil can also trick you into self-righteousness. Being self-righteous is just as bad as being in sin. If you have to tell people that you're serving God and tell them how spiritual you are, then you're not spiritual. All of these things bring condemnation and shame, which bring fear to our hearts and cause us to question whether or not Jesus answers our prayers and fulfills His promises in our lives.

I still have to work on trusting God sometimes. All of us do from time to time. We've been hurt, abused, rejected, and have suspicions about people. But when these doubts come, you need to let them go. Let that hurt go. Even though I'm a preacher, I'm a normal person. I have normal fights with the devil on my hands. But as long as you and I keep ourselves built up by praying in the Holy Ghost and keep our minds renewed, we will stay free in the love of God.

You see, I am free to receive God's unconditional love and blessings because my heart has come to believe the truth. The Scripture says, "There is therefore now no condemnation to those who are in Christ Jesus. For whom He foreknew, He also predestined to be conformed to the image of His Son"(Romans 8:1, 29, NKJV). Do you understand that—we are to be conformed to the image of Jesus Christ?!

This passage from Romans goes on to say, "Moreover whom He predestined, these He also called; whom He called, these He also justified; and whom He justified, these He also glorified. What then shall we say to these things? If God is for us, who can be against us? He who did not spare His own Son, but delivered Him up for us all, how shall He not with Him also freely give us all things? Who shall bring a charge against God's elect? It is God who justifies. Who is he who condemns? It is Christ who died, and furthermore is also risen, who is even at the right hand of God, who also makes intercession for us." (Romans 8:30-34, NKJV).

I'm going to start using legal terms because we are going into the court room in this scripture. Notice that the writer asks, "Who shall bring a charge against God's elect?" The fact is, it is God who justifies, who puts us in right relationship to Himself. Who shall come forward and accuse or impeach those whom God has chosen? It is God who acquits us! Who is there to condemn us? Christ Jesus, who was raised from the dead and now sits at the right hand of God, is actually interceding for us!

Maybe you're a soulwinner, a teacher or a student, and in your heart you love Jesus and worship Him and like to serve Him, but have a problem. Maybe you have perversion in your mind and you can't stay off the Internet pornography sites, or maybe you can't stop doing things in secret that are sinful or maybe you can't stop gossiping. Maybe you manipulate people or maybe you struggle with an eating disorder. Maybe you say vulgar things or maybe you are dishonest and deceptive. Can these things separate you from the love of God?

Notice what Scripture says, "For I am persuaded that neither death nor life, nor angels nor principalities nor powers, nor things present nor things to come, nor height nor depth, nor any other created thing, shall be able to separate us from the love of God which is in Christ Jesus our Lord" (Romans 8:38-39, NKJV). Nothing shall separate us from God's love! Death can't, life can't, the angels can't and the demons can't. Our fears today, our worries about tomorrow, even the powers of hell can't keep God's love away from you.

I'm not going to say that the grace of God forgives everything automatically because people may think, "It's already forgiven. I can do what I want." That is not what

I'm saying. With any sin you may commit in the future, you can't just commit sin and say, "Oh God, forgive me," and then keep doing it again and again. God knows whether we are serious when we ask for forgiveness. If we keep doing that, then we're in a sinful state and we're not even saved—if we intentionally continue in our sin.

But if we have truly repented of our sin and turned from it, no one can bring condemnation on us. These verses from Romans 8 tell us that whether we are high in the sky or in the deepest ocean, nothing in all creation will ever be able to separate us from the love of God that is revealed in Christ Jesus. When I read that, I just want to stop and go, "Whew!" Nothing—not what you say to me or about me, how you react, how mad you may get at me – nothing can separate me from the love of God. That makes me free!

Jesus made it possible for us to live abundantly free from shame and condemnation by receiving the Heavenly Father's unconditional love and His good opinion toward us. I guarantee you that I'm not perfect, but it doesn't matter. God loves me and nothing can separate me from that love.

You might catch me on an off day. We all have our off days. I might have just had a rough counseling session with somebody or maybe have just hung up from a rough phone conversation and I might react. But I guarantee you that right after that, I will get on my knees and say, "Oh God, help me. I'm angry and I'm tired." If you are hungry, angry, lonely, or tired, these are the things the devil watches for in your life to trip you up. But if you acknowledge your weaknesses and cry to God for forgiveness and help, no one can bring a charge against you. You see, if our Heavenly Father, the King of kings, judges us justified, acquitted, innocent, and righteous, then no other judgment matters. God is the final authority in my life and your life and what He says about us is true.

Romans 8:34 tells us that Jesus is sitting at the right hand of the Father, actually pleading our case for us. Jesus is your advocate. The Bible says, "My little children, I write you these things so that you may not violate God's law and sin. But if anyone should sin, we have an Advocate (One Who will intercede for us)" (1 John 2:1-2, AMP).

Every time you entertain a perverted thought, He will intercede for you. If you're sneaking around going to bed with people, drinking, doing drugs, and doing things with your body nobody knows about but you, He is interceding for you. You see, you can't ever hide all this stuff. God sees everything. You may think you're hiding and getting away with it, but nothing escapes the watchful eye of God. The good news is, we have an advocate with the Father and He's Jesus Christ, the righteous one who conforms to the Father's will in every purpose, thought, and action. That same Jesus is our propitiation. What does that mean? He is the atoning sacrifice for our sins and not for ours alone, but for the sins of the whole world.

Now, the Apostle John is admonishing you in this verse not

to sin, but if you do sin, know that Jesus is at the right hand of the Father interceding for you. His sacrifice was enough to free you from condemnation, even when you fail. Thank God!

Always, at the end of the day, I examine my day and I say, "I could have done that differently, Lord." But when I do that, He constantly reminds me that I am righteous in Him. One day, I was asking for a deeper revelation of the truth that I can be righteous in Him. He helped me understand what it means for Jesus to be sitting at the right hand of the Father interceding on my behalf.

I said to God, "I want to know exactly what it means for Jesus to be sitting at Your right hand interceding for me. I want You to put me there, just like when You gave me a revelation of blind Bartimaeus sitting on the highway begging. You gave me a revelation so real, I actually tasted the dust in my mouth as I heard him crying, 'Jesus, thou Son of David, have mercy on me.' I won't ever forget that. I want the revelation to be as clear as when you showed me the woman with the issue of blood. I had a revelation of how she felt and how her faith became so strong that even though she just barely touched the hem of Jesus' garment, she received her healing. I want to see what it means for Jesus to be at Your right hand interceding on my behalf."

I want to share with you what God revealed to me in response to my plea. The Father is a righteous judge. The Bible says that the devil is your accuser. Jesus is your defense attorney. He sits at the right hand of the Father, interceding for you, and you're seated with Him. You're seated on the witness stand and the devil is the prosecuting attorney, throwing every fiery dart of accusation at your heart. The devil takes the law, the very Word of God, and begins to accuse you saying, "You are not righteous. The law says you have to perfectly keep all of God's commands in order to be declared righteous. You have failed so many times. You don't even come close to measuring up."

Jesus sits at the right hand of the Father. He pleads your case. He says to you, "I am the atoning sacrifice for all your sins. The law could never make you righteous. I love you so much that I died and rose again so that you could be declared righteous in Me. I have fulfilled the law for you and given you My righteousness as a gift of grace. You're righteous because of your faith in Me, not because of anything you do, how you live or what you've been taught in the past."

We get this so messed up in our minds. We think our righteousness comes from how we've been raised, what we came out of, what we've done or witnessed. The truth is, you are righteous because of your faith in Jesus, and that's the only reason you are righteous. In the court of Heaven, the Father slams down His gavel on the desk and boldly stares at you saying, "You have been declared righteous in My sight, not because you obeyed the law perfectly, but because you have placed your faith in My Son, Jesus."

The devil may try to speak to your heart again with another accusation. He may say, "There are many conditions to God's promises and you have not met them all. The law says you have to obey all of God's commandments perfectly, in order to be blessed by Him." The devil is taking God's Word and misrepresenting it! He's throwing words from Deuteronomy 28:1-14 at you. Now we all know we have failed to meet this condition. By what we have done ourselves, we do not qualify for God's promised blessings.

Jesus, your Advocate, steps up to your defense again and He says, "You're no longer a slave to the law and its demands on you. You are my Father's beloved child and an heir to all His promises. You qualify for all My Father's promises because you have been made righteous through your faith in Me."

God's Word says, "But when the fullness of the time was come, God sent forth his Son, made of a woman, made under the law, To redeem them that were under the law, that we might receive the adoption of sons. And because ye are sons, (you're not a slave, you're a son or daughter) God hath sent forth the Spirit of his Son into your hearts, crying, Abba, Father. Wherefore thou art no more a servant, but a son; and if a son, then an heir of God through Christ" (Galatians 4:4-, interpretation in parenthesis mine).

The Father slams down His gavel on His desk again. He says to you, "You're my beloved child and everything I have belongs to you. My promised blessings are yours. They are yes and amen in your life because you are in My Son Jesus."

Just like with the temptation of Jesus in the wilderness (Matthew 4:1-11), the devil may try to come at you one more time. He may make one more attempt to accuse you and fill your heart with condemnation. He'll look at you and say, "You're guilty of many sins, even when you claim to be walking with Christ. Yesterday, you argued with your spouse and you were impatient with your children. You've made many poor choices in the past. The law says in Deuteronomy 28:15-66, if you don't obey every commandment of God, you'll be cursed. You deserve the curse and must pay for your sins."

Jesus Christ stands to His feet and says, "You know, I purchased your freedom from the curse." Remember that. There are generational devils that hover you. It's up to you to accept or reject that falsehood. You're the one who has a choice. Jesus Christ purchased your freedom from the curse of the law by becoming a curse for you. Your sins are forgiven and you're abundantly free from all penalty and punishments (Ephesians 1:7). You're free from condemnation because of your faith in Christ The Father slams down His gavel one last time and forever declares to you, "I don't remember a sin you ever committed (Hebrews 8:12). I have established a new covenant and because of your faith in My Son Jesus, I judge you forgiven, justified, innocent, acquitted, and righteous in Him. There is no condemnation for you because you are in My Son, Christ Jesus."

This is the revelation God gave me of how Jesus intercedes for us. The Father, Son, and Holy Spirit all agree that you've been made righteous. You must make up your mind that you're not going to compromise on anything. Accept the righteousness Christ has purchased for you.

Now, we still need to watch how we talk to our spouse. Watch how we talk to our children. You're not perfect. I'm not perfect. We need to watch how we talk to each other. We've got to love each other. We all get impatient, run off at the mouth, and have to ask forgiveness for our actions. But we are not condemned. Do not accept the condemnation the devil will try to throw at you!

For many years in my Christian life, my heart was filled with shame because of the things I did that I'm not proud of. I struggled with discouragement and disappointment because of the devil's accusations against me. He spoke lies to my heart: "You don't deserve a happy marriage because of the sin that you've committed and the lies you've told. You lied so much when you were growing up. You don't deserve a happy marriage. You're going to pay for your sins. God won't bless your marriage. You didn't have any examples of a godly marriage. How are you going to bless your marriage? You had no examples to follow."

For the longest time, I relied on my husband to get me through these times of accusation. Bobby would sit me down and say, "You don't have to have an example to follow. We make this marriage. You're not a disappointment. You're a good wife." He constantly had to build me up. You will wear out your spouse if you have to have them constantly build you up. If you stayed built up in Jesus, you wouldn't have to have anybody else build you up.

You see, the devil comes with guilt and condemnation and follows you around, trying to get you to accept his accusations. Do you see how a Christian, even though they have been set free and forgiven and justified, can let the devil's lies come at them? It wasn't until I finally cried out, "Jesus, I want You to show me the truth that will set me free," that the Holy Spirit began to give me a revelation of God's love and grace.

God spoke to my heart and said, "Zona, I declare you justified. Your sins are forgiven and forgotten. I made you righteous and worthy of all My promised blessings through your faith, and not because of whose daughter you are, not because of how many sermons you've preached, not because of how many people you've fed in the soup kitchen or how many students you have. It's not because of how many people are in the church or how much you do. I made you righteous and worthy of all My promised blessings through your faith in My Son Jesus. I paid the price for you, so you could live loved. I paid the price for you to live free!"

So how can we live free from our past mistakes? Look at what the Lord says in His Word. He tells us to forget the former things. Don't dwell on the past. Don't ever mention it again, unless it's to train a child. The scripture continues, "I, even I, am He who blots out your transgressions for My own sake; And I will not remember your sins" (Isaiah 43:18, 25, NKJV). In another scripture, He tells us that He has swept away our sin like the morning mist. He has scattered our offenses like the cloud. He tells us to return to Him, for He has paid the price to set us free (Isaiah 44:22).

We've got to wake up to the truth of God's Word and the power of His love. We have to keep ourselves built up by praying in tongues. We have to keep our minds renewed by reading the Word.

At one time, I surrendered to the lies I had been told. I believed the lies the devil was telling me. I really thought that the health problems I was experiencing came because I had stopped my field ministry and didn't go out as much. But God was so good to send people into my life to help me and pray for me. He was so good to give me a revelation of His love. He met me where my faith was. Why? Because He loves me so much.

When I surrendered myself to the truth of God's Word and to His great love, things began to change gradually. The Lord did not do a quick work in me. He gave me the revelation of what He went through when He was sent to the cross. He gave me a revelation of the blood of Jesus and the great love that brought that sacrifice. The more

I thought upon the truth of who I am in Christ Jesus and His great love for me, the more freedom I began to experience. God in His great love set me free.

I find myself experiencing the blessing of God on my life as I agree with the One who loves me. The same can be true for you. God's grace, brought about because of His love, can set you free and bring every blessing to your life. Seek after a revelation of that love and prepare to experience God's best in your life.

# ABOUT THE AUTHOR

Zona Hayes-Morrow lives in Cleveland, Tennessee, with her husband and daughter where she is the Director of New Life Bible College, Chief of Staff for Norvel Hayes Ministries, and Senior Pastor of New Life Bible Church.

When not busy fulfilling these responsibilities, Zona is traveling and ministering where the Lord leads her. She has a tremendous testimony of how the Lord has healed her from numerous diseases such as lupus and kidney failure. Her burden to see God's power set people free, while meeting their needs, is shown in her everyday life as well as in her ministry.

# PRAYER OF SALVATION

God loves you—no matter who you are, no matter what your past. God loves you so much that He gave His one and only begotten Son for you. The Bible tells us that "...whoever believes in Him shall not perish but have eternal life" (John 3:16 NIV). Jesus laid down His life and rose again so that we could spend eternity with Him in heaven and experience His absolute best on earth. If you would like to receive Jesus into your life, say the following prayer out loud and mean it from your heart.

*Heavenly Father, I come to You admitting that I am a sinner. Right now, I choose to turn away from sin, and I ask You to cleanse me of all unrighteousness. I believe that Your Son, Jesus, died on the cross to take away my sins. I also believe that He rose again from the dead so that I might be forgiven of my sins and made righteous through faith in Him. I call upon the name of Jesus Christ to be the Savior and Lord of my life. Jesus, I choose to follow You and ask that You fill me with the power of the Holy Spirit. I declare that right now I am a child of God. I am free from sin and full of the righteousness of God. I am saved in Jesus' name. Amen.*

If you prayed this prayer to receive Jesus Christ as your Savior for the first time, please contact us on the Web at **www.harrisonhouse.com** to receive a free book.

Or you may write to us at

**Harrison House** • P.O. Box 35035 • Tulsa, Oklahoma 74153

# The Harrison House Vision

Proclaiming the truth and the power

Of the Gospel of Jesus Christ

With excellence;

Challenging Christians to

Live victoriously,

Grow spiritually,

Know God intimately.